A Crisis of Heart & Hope

A Premature Birth Spiritual Care Guide for Parents, Families and Caregivers

Sharon Beshoar

LIFETIME CHRONICLE PRESS/dba
LONDON PUBLISHING
Montrose, CO

First edition
Printed in the United States of America

Library of Congress Control Number: 2011935306
ISBN: 978-0-9822935-9-1

Cover and book design by Laurie Goralka Design
Illustrations by Kevin F. Novack
Visit Kevin on his Facebook page at Kevin F. Novack Fine Art

London Publishing
10614 Bostwick Park Rd.
Montrose, CO 81401
970-240-1153
chronicle@montrose.net
www.londonpublishing.net

Work of the eyes is done,
now go and do heart work
on all the images imprisoned within you.

—*Turning Point* by RAINER MARIA RILKE

DEDICATION

For Preemies Everywhere—Lives to be *Celebrated*

Royal state has been yours from birth,
from the womb of the morning like dew,
your strength will come to you.
—PSALMS 110:3

In honor of Our Mother of Perpetual Help

ACKNOWLEDGEMENTS

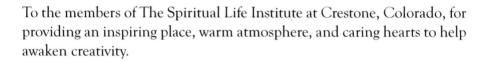

To the members of The Spiritual Life Institute at Crestone, Colorado, for providing an inspiring place, warm atmosphere, and caring hearts to help awaken creativity.

To neonatal medical staffs everywhere, whose work is a continuation of God's amazing birthing process.

To my Friends on the Journey, for their patience and understanding. For Janet Oslund and Karen Nickolson, friends with seeker's spirits and gracious hearts, for their help, expertise, and encouragement.

Last, but foremost, to my family. With special thanks to my son, daughter-in-law, and husband for sharing their stories. And to the rest of my family, this book would never have been written without each and every one of you. I hold *all* of you tenderly, passionately, and lovingly in my heart—*always*.

SPECIAL ACKNOWLEDGEMENTS

Grateful acknowledgement is made to the following publishers and/or authors who have granted permission. The titles of their work are listed in the order in which the material appears in this book.

Lights of Passage by Kathleen Wall and Gary Ferguson, reprinted with permission of HarperCollins Publishers.

The Heart Knows by Kathy Sherman, CSJ., reprinted with permission of the Sisters of St. Joseph of La Grange, IL.

Reprinted by permission of SSL/Sterling Lord Literistic, Inc. From *Crow and Weasel*, Copyright 1990 by Barry Lopez.

Jeffrey's Poem © Garrison Keillor. Used with permission. All rights reserved.

Night Nurse words and music by Gregory Isaacs and Sylvester Weise
Copyright © 1982 CHARISMA MUSIC PUBLISHING CO. LTD. and
    SPLASH DOWN MUSIC
All Rights for CHARISMA MUSIC PUBLISHING CO. LTD. in the U.S. and Canada Controlled and Administered by EMI APRIL MUSIC INC.
All Rights Reserved International Copyright Secured Used by Permission
Reprinted by permission of Hal Leonard Corporation.

Grandchildren Are So Much Fun We Should Have Them First by Gene Perret. Reprinted with permission of the author.

William from WHITE PINE; POEMS AND PROSE POEMS, copyright © 1994 by Mary Oliver, reprinted by permission of Houghton Mifflin Harcourt Publishing Company.

Psalm 139 by Maureen Leach OSF, and Nancy Schreck, OSF, from *Psalms Anew*, Reprinted with permission of the authors.

Preemie Purple Heart by Renae Ericson, www.preemiepurpleheart.com, reprinted with permission of the author.

For Baby (For Bobbie) words and music by JOHN DENVER Copyright © 1965; Renewed 1993 BMG Ruby Songs (ASCAP) and FSMGI (IMRO); and CHERRY LANE MUSIC PUBLISHING COMPANY, INC. (ASCAP) All rights for FSMGI (IMRO) Administered by Chrysalis One Music (ASCAP) International Copyright Secured
Reprinted by permission of Hal Leonard Corporation
All Rights Reserved   Used by Permission

Newborn Fingers from FINGERS ARE ALWAYS BRINGING ME NEWS by Mary O'Neill. Copyright ©1969 Mary O'Neill. © Renewed 1997 by Abigail Hagler and Erin Baroni. Used by permission of Marian Reiner.

Patience from *Collected and New Poems 1924-1963* by Mark Van Doren. Copyright © 1963 by Mark Van Doren. Copyright renewed 1991 by Dorothy G. Van Doren. Reprinted by permission of Hill and Wang, a division of Farrar, Straus and Giroux. LLC.

Hope from *Alive Together, New and Selected Poems* by Lisel Mueller. Reprinted by permission of Louisiana State University Press.

The author wishes to thank the Crisis Publishing Co., Inc. the publisher of the magazine of the National Association for the Advancement of Colored People, for the use of *The Negro Speaks of Rivers* by Langston Hughes, first published in the June 1921 issue of *The Crisis*.

...the Mother Struggles with Regret, And Then We Smell the Cool Damp of the Creek, Recovery, Mystery at the Door, During the Breathing Meditation, Breathing and Microcosm by Rosemerry Wahtola Trommer, copyright © by the author, reprinted with permission of the author, www.ahundredfallingveils.wordpress.com.

CONTENTS

INTRODUCTION

Hope is a thing with feathers
That perches in the soul.
And sings the tune
Without words,
and never stops at all.
—EMILY DICKINSON

*I*f you are reading this book, you undoubtedly already know the surprise and shock of a premature birth, a heart-wrenching and frightening experience, especially for parents. The hopes and dreams of bringing a rosy, healthy baby into the world are supplanted by fear and uncertainty about what the future may hold. The birth affects not only the parents but also siblings and extended family members, who are at a loss as to what to expect or how to respond in a helpful manner.

Whether the child is very small or just a few weeks premature, the mother and father are deluged with unfamiliar and seemingly menacing medical terminology, particular conditions or problems that are affecting the child's body, or a possible need for future surgery. To the uninformed eye, the baby looks vulnerable and extremely fragile. The mother is faced with the unique challenge of integrating the needs of a premature child with her own bodily changes following the birth. Sometimes she might also be healing after surgery. She will not have the age-old advantage of holding her child right away and nursing it. This separation anxiety in itself is enough to cause very low spirits in many new moms or postpartum depression in a few.

At this uncertain and frightening time, it is the highly skilled and caring medical staffs in hospitals who take the lead in directing the baby's care. Based on their training and experience, doctors and nurses set into motion the procedures to help the premature child develop fully functioning systems. They examine the baby's brain, heart, eyes, and lungs frequently, and they constantly monitor the child's temperature, oxygen levels, hydration, nourishment, and weight.

Although parents are integrated into the baby's care as much as possible, they are still frequently overwhelmed by their own fears and by the intense activity, alternating with long periods of waiting, which surrounds their child. It is the emotional and spiritual needs of the parents, family, and friends at this time that this book speaks to primarily. In the whirlwind of activities and treatments and the ups and downs of the baby's progress, the parents must deal with their own worries, grief, fear, and other strong emotions. The goal of this book is to help parents find comfort, peace, and hope so that they may be able to better care for their beloved child.

My own family's experience began late on a cold December day in 2004. Several days later, one of my grandchildren was born far from home and very prematurely at 1 lb. 13 oz. I immediately had a desperate fear for his life, and then had to watch the alarm and agony of my son and daughter-in-law as they tried to adjust to the reality of long-term hospitalization or worse for their son.

When our parish, where I had worked for sixteen years, went from two full-time clergy to one, I was invited to move from the front office to a leadership position with an administrative and ministerial focus. As a result, I returned to school and obtained my master's degree which had a pastoral care emphasis. My new duties had a birth-to-death focus, and I entered people's lives on a much deeper and more intimate level. I have held the hand of a new mother who was weeping her heart out at the death of her full-term baby daughter, and had long conversations with another new mom whose son was stillborn eight months into the pregnancy. I have prayed over the lifeless body of a six- year-old child who was taken in a tragic accident, as his parents were desperately trying to cope with their horror in the adjoining room. I then sat for a long time with these same parents who were desperate for the return of our priest. These and a myriad of ministerial experiences, plus my longtime passionate belief in the God of all peoples, a benevolent Cosmic Creator, have given me the strength and determination to proceed with this book.

Though I had considerable experience ministering to patients and families in hospital settings and had spent hours in intensive care units,

I was quite unprepared for the neonatal intensive care unit (NICU) that held my own flesh and blood. I hoped that my children would receive top-quality spiritual attention so that the whole family's care would be truly holistic. It was very troubling to me that some of the things that occurred resulted in making their spiritual care experience a negative one.

In addition to being a guide to the parents and families of premature infants, this book is offered as a supplement to what the doctors and nurses who work in NICUs do. They are among the most special people in the world and are unheralded heroes, heroines, and saints. Without them, many a family's story would turn out quite differently.

Professional spiritual caregivers and perhaps some hospital chaplains might also benefit from this book. Chaplains and family members—many of whom have never gone through a birth experience, much less a traumatic one—can learn from this book so they may offer the new parents more authentic spiritual care, or at least be a small part of their own family's support systems. They may also learn techniques to suggest so that the parents can nurture themselves as well as their child.

This book is organized into two parts. The first section offers suggestions for parents for meeting their emotional and spiritual needs as they spend long days and nights in the hospital, learning how to welcome their tiny child. Focusing on relaxation and exercise, music and poetry, nature, or meditation and prayer can help develop a well-integrated perspective for dealing with the unknown. In addition, ritual is explained as a way in which many of these practices can come together in a powerful and helpful way. Ritual allows parents and other family members to formally acknowledge their experiences, such as through a ceremony for welcoming the child into the home when that blessed day arrives.

The second part of the book points out the importance of storytelling and relates the story of our family's experience described from the perspective of the mother, the father, the grandmother, and the grandfather. We offer these stories because they provide a way for people to understand the profound effect a premature birth has, and to glimpse the possibility of ways to cope with their unknown future. In addition, on the flip side of this book, there is a children's storybook in which the baby tells his own story. This perspective will help siblings and young friends better understand this unusual and sometimes scary event.

Read this book in any order that makes sense to you personally; feel free to begin with Part Two or with the baby's story. Dig into the appendixes for whatever you can use. If you are a new parent, you might find yourself especially drawn to one or two chapters of Part One. If so, these could be the areas in which your spirit is feeling more at home. It is my desire that you will feel you have been helped because your own worries and fears have been recognized and gently cradled. In the days and weeks to come, look for your experiences to be filled with many small "feathers of hope" that drift through the air and fall gently upon your hearts. May you forever remember this entire birth experience as a sacred time.

If you are a family member, there might be new ideas here to help you give support. May you read the book with a sense of peace, comfort, and hope that all will be well at the end of this truly incredible journey. If you are a spiritual caregiver, there might be ways to help you become a better vessel through which the reality of a loving and caring God flows. However the parts of this volume are used, may the goodness that is always available in the universe shine through into the lives of families of prematurely born infants.

PART ONE:

Nuturing the Spiritual

CARE AND THE SPIRIT

A wounded spirit who can bear?
—PROVERBS 18:14

I know all about the ways of the heart—how it wants to be alive.
—RUMI

Although crises come in many different forms, universally they make us question and seek answers. They cause anguish, worry, and sometimes unbelievable emotional pain. The premature birth of one's baby is just such a happening. Most parents who experience having a tiny child who cannot survive on its own fortunately receive high-quality medical care for both the mother and child. Medical teams of doctors and nurses who specialize in neonatal care are highly skilled, dedicated, and caring individuals. They recognize and respect the emotional turmoil that a premature birth causes and do as much as possible to give good, comprehensive medical information to parents while showing patience and compassion as they teach the new mom and dad how to interact with and help care for their tiny, vulnerable child.

But amidst this wealth of physical and educational help, where does the emotional and spiritual care come from? The medical professionals often give great emotional support. Hospital chaplains are generally relied upon to provide the spiritual perspective for parents who have just received a wake-up call unlike anything they ever dreamed possible. When called upon to do so, chaplains contact the parents and find out what their needs are. What happens next is different with every family and is much more diversified than the medical care provided. The chaplain's support is tailored to the religious background of the parent or family. Sometimes this care is very good, at times it is only adequate, and at other times it lacks meaning or is a negative experience.

Some people recognize their spiritual nature; to others, it remains veiled and completely hidden. The word *spiritual* comes from the Latin word *spiritualis*, meaning "of breathing or air." One simple way to look at spirituality is that it's something that maintains life and comes from deep inside a person. Traditionally, the spirit has been thought of as something unidentifiable and intangible but definitely separate from the material world and the body. Many religions identify this something as soul.

Some religions and many people who have never embraced any particular religious tradition believe that there is a separate spirit world filled with beings without a body. For example, Christians believe that after the death of the body on this earth, the spirit remains alive in heaven. Other people hold no such beliefs but might agree that qualities of the spirit could be identified as a human being's ability to delve deeply within her or himself and draw on inner resources, energies, and strengths. Most people would agree that the core unifying principles of empathy, compassion, a sense of oneness, and love transcend the boundaries of religious dogma. This ability of the spirit is most often activated and recognized in times of crisis; when hope is brought alive and can be a constant source of comfort.

Effective spiritual guidance requires open and honest communication between the parent and the caregiver. For example, often the conversation between the parents and the chaplain begins with a simple question such as, "How are you doing today?" This may provide opportunity to discuss emotions and fears or how the parents have coped with difficult situations in the past. It is certainly a chance to show interest and compassion.

From there, depending on what he or she hears, the chaplain could suggest appropriate ways for the parents to deal with their stresses, such as exercise, time in nature, formal prayer, and the other suggestions offered in this book. In the next weeks, the discussion could move to a different level or another perspective, depending on the parents' needs. No such thing happened with the priest who came to baptize my grandchild; he did not even return for a repeat visit during the months the baby was in the hospital, though various chaplains on hospital staff did drop by occasionally at first. On their part, the parents must be proactive about their own spiritual care.

To achieve optimum psycho-emotional-physical well-being, a person and his or her spiritual guide must acknowledge all aspects of his or her being: the body, mind, and spirit must be in tune. If one dimension is ignored, the others will suffer. Holistic healing acknowledges that it is not only the hospital professionals who heal; they are often just the catalysts. They have the ability to stimulate the spirit within, enabling all aspects of the person to function in harmony. How the parents embrace this stimulus is up to them, of course.

Sometimes parents do not wish to see a chaplain or any religious representative because their beliefs are not shaped along those pathways. But they still need some sort of psycho-emotional support, and it is important that they be provided with a place or a circumstance to give words to the troubling experience they have been forced to live through, so they do not continue to feel confused and suffocated by it.

All adult persons want to be in control of their own lives, at least so that they can stay on a comfortable and healthy plane. When a premature birth suddenly occurs, parents lose control of their lives. In that powerful emotional state, they may express desperation, disappointment, loss, anxiety, anger, helplessness, devastation, fear, shock, agitation, or other emotions. They might be paralyzed by feelings of grief and be unable to comfort one another.

Conscious spiritual care of some kind will slowly reawaken feelings of release and give parents the ability to believe that comfort and happiness are really possible in their future. Many activities can facilitate peace and a sense of release or well-being, awakening deep hope.

Relaxation and Exercise

He that can rest is greater than he that can take cities.
—Benjamin Franklin

Walking is the best possible exercise.
Habituate yourself to walk far.
—Thomas Jefferson

Needless to say, the early days and weeks of a preemie's life are a tense time for parents. Tension is silent and insidious and can be as destructive as a virus or a slow-growing cancer. It can harm one's body and might cause or aggravate disease. It causes changes in body tissues, the digestive system, and blood vessels. A brain affected by anxiety or anger can be rendered incapable of putting rational thoughts together, much less making good decisions. The brain is much like a computer that makes muscles work in a coordinated, proper manner. When nervous tension disrupts this flow, the body is vulnerable to damage.

Fortunately my family did not develop any physical illness, but my son and daughter-in-law lived with deep stress and strain during their four-month stay in Denver. I spent five days there immediately following the birth and witnessed emotion-packed verbal exchanges. For example, unspoken fear and frustration were vented through impatient words about breast pumping and the baby's nourishment. My son left his part-time job behind when the birth happened so he could be part of the daily care of his new baby. He was planning to return to school to get his teaching certificate in the near future also, so he used the time to choose the college and firm up things with them. My daughter-in-law left her classroom of second graders and knew that she had only so much maternity leave to count on. This increased their financial worries, though my son and I discussed this only once. It was a very good thing that these new parents were offered privileges at a gym located in the hospital. They used it often to exercise, which relieved stress and helped them to relax.

Relaxation is one of the most important things a person can do to immunize against the debilitating effects of tension. There are many emotional benefits to mastering the art of relaxation, but the physical benefits are important also. Muscles work better and move with more fluidity and ease. Blood vessels function better to help the blood deliver ample amounts of oxygen to both muscles and the brain. Relaxation balances the input and expenditure of oxygen in our muscles. This balance helps release tension or anxiety and calms both the body and the spirit. The question is not if parents of a prematurely born infant need to relax, but rather when in the sometimes frantic pace are they going to find the time to do it, and how will they approach it?

The ideal time for conscious relaxation activity is a matter of individual preferences and schedules. Any time during the day is fine, but it helps greatly to set a routine, commit to it, and stick with it as religiously as possible. One person might choose to rise early and take a half-hour walk or bike ride in a nearby park. Another might routinely take a hot soaking bath, water laced with herbal supplements to enhance relaxation. Yet a different person might find his best relaxation in immersing himself in music. Someone else might find relaxation in escaping into a good book.

Journaling is another effective therapeutic activity. Writing down concerns gets them out of one's head and releases some pent-up anxiety. While my son, daughter-in-law, and new grandchild were so far away from home, I kept a journal that I wrote in each day. I moved on to creating a photo album that held some of the words from the journal, pictures, poems, and things symbolic to this fragile new life. This was something I could share with concerned friends, and it provided me release of my anxiety. I also spent many hours walking a riverside pathway in the cold winter air.

Certain kinds of exercise—leisurely walking and stretching but not competitive sports—are particularly relaxing. With gentle exercise, muscles contract and then relax, creating a cycle that produces tranquilizing chemicals called "endorphins," which are both relaxants and painkillers. Exercise also produces an electrical effect on the neurological connections in the muscles, which causes them to relax. Physical trainers agree that stretching is the best kind of exercise for relaxation, and it is a must before other more strenuous forms of exercise.

Exercise that is done sensibly, slowly, and progressively is always beneficial. Moderate exercise helps a person's overall condition by lowering blood pressure and improving flexibility and digestion. New parents should include therapeutic exercise to reduce stress and maintain good health. Their routine should also include eating nutritious food, drinking lots of water, getting sufficient sleep, and consuming no more than two alcoholic drinks a day.

Often, I find that inspiration comes to me when I am putting in my miles on the treadmill. I feel as if things are flowing well enough in my body that both my mind and spirit have been awakened and have integrated with it. This inspiration might be just an idea for a unique dinner that evening or remembering an old friend's maiden name. But it also might be solving a serious problem that had been niggling at me for a long time, such as how to find just the right words or an action that would help a hurting friend. Or it could be finding new insight about a broken relationship that might be an important step toward healing.

The new mother's exercise regimen might differ drastically from the father's routine. Start with your doctor's recommendations; make a commitment to a plan that includes setting goals and keeping track of certain parameters, such as type of activity and its intensity and duration. Begin slowly and progress gradually. You might invest in a pedometer to determine a baseline, and then set a goal to increase your steps 500 to a thousand per day until you reach 10,000 steps a day, the American College of Sports Medicine's recommendation for healthy people.

Mind-body exercises such as yoga are extremely helpful for relieving stress. Such activity helps unite the mind and body, thus restoring emotional and physiological balance. Some postures in yoga are thought to enhance mental and emotional health. A professional massage or a facial are other means of enhancing relaxation.

Water, especially moving water, is an effective way of relieving tension. Water has a healing effect. Since I have lived in a mountainous region all my life, I find my healing water in rivers and creeks, but ocean settings would provide much the same emotional therapy.

Rivers and oceans are filled with life and energy because of their constantly moving, changing, and reforming conditions. Their waters provide nourishing and cleansing realities for our bodies and spirits. I have spent many hours in a canoe on rivers (or on lakes when a river was not easy to access), feeling the soothing motion of the water wash away tensions, hurts, and stresses. On the banks of the Flathead River in Montana, I performed a ritual of transition as one professional phase of my life ended and I yearned to move into a new job where I could still use my gifts and experience in service to others. Because my life's direction was changing, it was significant to me that this river had three forks, two of which my husband and I had canoed that summer. I have sat in meditative prayer along the banks of many different rivers and creeks over the past thirty years, seeking release of burdens and insight into my future. Much more routinely, walks along rivers provide me with emotional release and healthful exercise.

There's an old Negro spiritual, perhaps Gullah in origin that suggests that many others have found healing solace in flowing water.

> *Gone down to the river,*
> *The river flows with life,*
> *Gone beg my God to help us all,*
> *Help us through our strife.*
>
> *Take this pain away, God!*
> *Oh, take our pain away!*
> *Heal our hearts so we can live,*
> *To praise You one more day!*

Flowing water has a primordial pull that is ancient and that courses through the depths of our bodies, minds, and spirits. Langston Hughes' poem, "The Negro Speaks of Rivers," is a beautiful piece that expresses how deeply water is connected with our spirits. He says that his soul has become deep like the rivers and speaks of his connection with his ancestral people through the river's water. This poem is included in Appendix B of this book.

Exercise activity or relaxation exercises might not provide optimum release and comfort if too much stress is pent up inside a person. The shedding of tears and the joy of laughter can aid in the release of anxiety.

Tears, Crying Out, and Laughter

Most men cry better than they speak.
—Henry David Thoreau

*It is requisite for relaxation of the mind that we make use,
from time to time, of playful deeds and jokes.*
—Thomas Aquinas

One of the most startlingly difficult and heart-wrenching things parents of the preemie baby have to deal with is hearing their baby's tiny cries. The parents themselves may have shed quite a few tears in the days surrounding the birth. When their child finds its wee voice for the first time and cries, their own emotions are fragile and near the surface. It is quite possible that they may engage in their first family cry-fest together! Tears are always healing. Mom and Dad shouldn't hesitate to let tears roll, because there is a therapeutic benefit in crying.

Unfortunately, because of social awkwardness, many men in our society don't feel comfortable crying in front of another person, but fortunately it is more acceptable for women to cry. Throughout history, tears have been highly valued as an expression of deep caring and love among adults. We know that babies cry to express hunger, discomfort, or emotional distress; they don't actually shed tears until they are around two months old, so crying is a distress signal for them.

It wasn't until months after the birth that my son told me of how hearing his tiny son's cries tore at his heart and how he had shed tears in the privacy of the NICU several times. I joined my daughter-in-law in tearful harmony a few times, but much later I learned that my daughter-in-law cried daily. I know that this was good for her, but it was sad that later on in their stay, it was a source of frustration for my son.

An interesting scientific fact about tears is that irritant tears, such as those caused by onion peeling, contain 98 percent water, whereas tears caused by emotions are both protein rich and toxin filled. Biochemist and pioneer tear researcher Dr. William H. Frey II did research years ago while Director of Psychiatry Research Laboratories at St. Paul-Ramsey Medical Center in Minnesota. His research showed clearly from a scientific perspective that, after a good emotional cry, the body is rid of some toxins. He believes that emotional crying should no longer be perceived as a weakness but embraced as valuable and healing. We feel better because we are emotionally and physically more relaxed. Crying can be curative and more healthful than holding the emotions in check.

For family members who may be dealing with a seemingly overly tearful mother, here's a word of advice: tears are very connected to hormones as well as emotions. Both are running rampant in the mother's body after giving birth. In addition, she might be recovering from surgery and experiencing pain and discomfort from that and from pumping breast milk for her infant. Have patience, patience, and more patience with her if her tears or crying episodes seem to last for weeks too long. Draw upon all your reserves of empathy. Don't tell her to "get over it!" but give her tender loving care as best you can. Understand that her tears are helping her emotionally and physically. She wants to get over it as much or more than you want her to, and she will, in time.

Be aware, however, that a small percentage of women suffer from postpartum depression. If Mom is listless, has no energy, loses her appetite, and cries several times a day, consult your doctor. She might need more help.

Just as tears are healing, laughter has a similar therapeutic effect, probably because both provide deep emotional release. A great deal of research by doctors and health care professionals shows the benefits of laughter. A hearty laugh acts much like a massage, giving the diaphragm, abdomen, heart, lungs, and even the liver beneficial exercise. Laughter also provides a great cardiovascular workout, especially if it's hearty laughter. Dr. William F. Fry, Jr., of Stanford University, states that alertness hormones are produced when a person laughs, which in turn causes the release of endorphins in the brain. Laughter decreases stress hormone levels, improves the immune system, promotes relaxation, lowers blood pressure, and acts as a natural antidepressant. Moreover, laughter carries no social stigma for men as crying does.

Most of us have had the experience of "laughing so hard that we cried." Do you remember how good you felt after such an episode? Laughter is good for us. When I was growing up, my family used to laugh together over the jokes on *Reader's Digest's* "Laughter Is the Best Medicine" page. And adults and children alike love the comics—for good reason. There is an old adage that humor is a great way to make the unbearable bearable, as the popularity of the long-running TV show "M*A*S*H" attests. One of my fondest memories is of my parents, my older sister and her husband, myself and my husband, and our seven children sitting around my parents' dinner table and laughing at the jokes and the verbal antics of my husband and brother-in-law. My parents and brother-in-law are now deceased, but I still celebrate them and the many, many tears of laughter that flowed that evening.

In today's world, the Internet is a great source for jokes and humor. Radio and TV, too, have some funny shows. A favorite of mine and my husband's is the annual joke show on public radio's "A Prairie Home Companion." The 1970s and 1980s were the heyday of great variety-comedy shows. Little did we know then how good they were for us physically and spiritually! I firmly believe that our world would be a better place if there were more family-oriented humor on the airways now.

In our family, Catholic jokes and Irish jokes are a conversation staple because laughing at oneself is healthy and refreshing. Around the dinner table, we often share anecdotes about family and friends, neighbors and coworkers, politics, the local judiciary, and travel experiences. The best and most memorable stories are the funny ones.

Although close family members of new parents might be so concerned about Mom, Dad, and the baby that they are afraid to be a source of humor, good friends can fill in. True friends will lighten the mood with funny anecdotes and stories. Friends with whom you are able to laugh are indispensable. Regular time away from the NICU to take in a good comedy movie or play, or to have dinner with light-hearted friends, will provide welcome relief. Saint Patrick's Day fell during my children's stay in Denver. It was one of several times they gathered with friends away from the hospital to have an evening of fun and laughter.

Meditation and Prayer

The greatest prayer is patience.
—Buddah

God is always there, if you feel wounded.
He kneels over this earth like a divine medic.
—Teresa of Avila

*T*hankfulness for the gift of life is a fundamental wellspring of all religion and it's a striking fact that every world religion sees patience as a way to know God. Despite their different views about who God is and how to contact that presence, most agree that peacefulness is the essence of spirituality. Peacefulness and gratitude lead the practitioner to greater strength, more illumination, and a higher plane.

Sitting for hours in the NICU with a preemie child provides the perfect setting for parents to embrace patience as never before. They have to be patient because the process of growth and well-being cannot be rushed. Instant gratification in this electronic age is the norm, with e-mails flying across the office, city, country, and world; with the click of a mouse providing answers to most any question; and with text messaging and cell phones at our fingertips. These can be good tools to share progress, but the reality is that there are not going to be instant results with the preemie child. What a perfect time for a parent to awaken to the concept of practicing patience! Patience can draw one inward toward greater wisdom. When one is forced into a situation where patience is a must, it can turn into a gift to be mined.

The great spiritual challenge is to transcend worry and anxiety and develop an attitude of hopefulness and confidence, and be grateful that there are so many wonderful, dedicated people on your child's team. If you are a person who prays regularly, great; if you are not, this may be a time to rethink its importance.

Tried and true prayer methods may bring comfort, and this is good. But for right now, try to look at prayer with different eyes. Use the word *prayer* as a concept that expresses an interior practice, a moving inward where you go to experience hope and pure, unconditional love within yourself. Seek the place where it is possible to cooperate with total goodness and peace.

Whether you believe in a named God, some sort of higher power, or angels, or your deceased and beloved grandfather watching over you, or the entire communion of saints, prayer lets you reach out to something greater than yourself in order to take hold of forgotten power. It is an acknowledgment that there is another world available to us that our linear minds cannot comprehend. Whatever or whomever you pray to, open yourself to receiving unconditional love and peace.

Prayer must be more than an intellectual exercise being voiced in the mind. I remember a definition of prayer drilled into me by the good Sisters when I was a child: "Prayer is lifting our minds and hearts up to God." The key to effective prayer is the heart. The heart part goes clear into the depth of one's inner being, including the emotions. Too many adults pray only with their minds and are fearful of involving their entire body in the experience. Prayer can be a friendly guide through the worried and anxious hours that your child spends in the NICU. The birth of a premature child launches families on a deeply emotional pilgrimage, and prayer is a unique way to help consecrate those hours and days.

There are non-traditional ways of looking at prayer that will help ease worries. Prayer can be a four-step process that you might use to travel a continual route throughout your being. These steps may even be documented in a journal, because writing is cathartic and healing for some people, as it has always been for me.

1. Identify your thoughts and look beyond them.

Ask yourself what you're worried about today. Be specific. For example, "Will the hole in my baby's heart require surgery?" Write in a journal about this question for awhile. Search for a greater meaning—for yourself, for your spouse, and other family members. Identify how this might hinder or further your own spiritual growth.

2. Live in the moment.

When you find yourself thinking anxiously about the future, bring yourself back to the present moment. Live in the present only. Frame positive thoughts. Tell yourself, "I am grateful for the help we're being given. It is enough for me to be happy today. Tomorrow will take care of itself." Put these thoughts down in writing if you're using a journal. In other words, consciously develop an attitude of gratitude and mentally stay in the moment.

3. Voice a prayer.

When you can't let go of worries, ask help from your own Sacred Source. It can be a simple, spontaneous prayer such as, "Release me from this anxiety, Spirit of Peace." Say it several times over or use it as a mantra many times throughout your day. Breathe deeply as you pray it. Following is an ancient loving kindness verse that might be helpful to pray often. Perhaps it would be helpful to paste it on your mirror and pray it morning and night as you brush your teeth. Pray it for yourself, then pray it for your baby.

> *May I be free of worry*
> *May I be well*
> *May I feel safe and at ease*
> *May I be at peace.*

Let your bond with the Spirit calm you and carry your worries away.

4. Seek the innermost spot within yourself.

Anxious thoughts reside in the peripheral layers of awareness, but a state of peacefulness and calm is in your true center. Finding this place requires going deep within. Begin by taking several long, strong breaths to release tension, and then find a comfortable sitting position. Continue breathing a little more deeply than usual and pace your breaths evenly. Just concentrate on your breathing for a period of time. Then create a visual image of going down, and further down, within to your very core or soul—to a place of calm comfort and peace. Try to sense a profound stillness there...focus upon a sublime peacefulness...it will grow as the focus remains. Sometimes I will begin such meditation with a piece of melodious, soft music combined with deep breathing. Other times I just begin with concentrating on my breathing and bodily relaxation, moving slowly from head to toes.

I believe in the God of all peoples and, more specifically, the Trinitarian God of Christianity, but when I approach prayer as meditation,

I often name God as "Yahweh." This has ancient Hebrew roots, being the most sacred name of God formed by the four consonants, YHVH, and is considered too holy to be spoken aloud. In recent years, the use of Yahweh as God's name has been revived by more denominations, and it is used in a melodious way in some contemporary Catholic music based on Old Testament scripture, which enhances my prayer life.

While my children were in Denver, I used this name as a mantra to help my concerns flow from my mind into the reality of Love. During those months when I prayed in a meditative manner, it was with lips slightly parted, the first syllable of this holy name formed on the deep intake of breath (Yah), then the second syllable (weh) on the deep out-flow of breath. This I repeated several times, letting my breath form the name in a wordless way. After a few moments of this, there would be only silence. When thoughts or words began to creep into my mind (as they will unless one is in a deep meditative state), I drove them away with one of these phrases:

Relax your expectations,
receive what is.

Live in the present moment,
hold on to hope.

Then I returned to concentrating on my breathing. These words were also hung from my bathroom mirror, were on the window sill above my kitchen sink, and were at eye level above my desk. I repeated them many other times during my day.

The atmosphere in the NICU does not lend itself well to this type of prayer, so a daily trip to the chapel might be helpful, because it is generally quiet, uncrowded, and would be a good place to meditate. Meditation produces a deep inner calm. Simply put, it is spiritually framing a mind-body practice and doing it routinely.

Parents of a preemie spend hours watching their child breathe with the help of medical equipment and hearing the monitoring of oxygen levels in the little body and brain of their baby. It should then not be such a long jump to consider your own breathing rhythm as a way to calm your spirit. You might be surprised to discover that there is a special breathing technique that provides a marvelous form of relaxation. With this deep-breathing method, your body position can enhance the depth of each breath. Standing or sitting in an upright, erect position with shoulders back will enhance the lung's capacity. When the diaphragm, which is located in the belly, is in the down position, the lungs are able to expand more. When the "belly is out," the diaphragm moves out. So following mother's childhood reminder to "hold your stomach in" will not enhance the deep-breathing technique. It takes practice to make one's stomach protrude each time a breath is taken, but that's when the relaxation effect will work best.

Our breath is the bridge between our voices and our minds. A combination of deep breathing and walking or stretching is a very effective means of relieving tension and anxiety, subtly guiding the entire body— mental and physical—into a more healthful, relaxed state.

It is always important to remember that, as a healthy person, you are in control of your own thoughts and moods, and you can pull yourself up from a low mood or away from worrisome thoughts. During World War II, a popular song written by Johnny Mercer and sung by Bing Crosby provided the nation with a positive phrase to use in the midst of a dreadful war and daily bad news. The refrain of the song was "accentuate the positive, eliminate the negative, latch on to the affirmative, and don't mess with Mister In-between." Making this verse, or something similar, your own while in the NICU might help you focus on the positive and become more hopeful. For some unknown reason, I was reminded of this refrain during the early months of 2005, and I even went online to listen to the complete old tune that I remembered from my mother singing it during my childhood. It helped me, as the refrain circled through my mind at unexpected times, drawing me away from worries and refocusing my thoughts in a hopeful manner.

Other forms of spiritual nourishment are readily available and greatly helpful. They are ancient, subtle tools that preemie parents might want to more consciously reincorporate into their lives. Reading poetry or listening to music can take one away from the worries of the moment and instill confidence and hope in the future.

Music and Poetry

Without music life would be a mistake.
—Friedrich Nietzsche

Poetry is the universal language which the heart holds with nature and itself.
—William Hazlitt

Music has a powerful influence on both humans and animals. Tribal societies and early civilizations incorporated music into their daily lives and religious ceremonies from ancient times. Socrates said that harmony and rhythm make their way into the inmost soul and take a strong hold upon it, imparting grace. Music has power over our spirits and can also be a moving influence upon the body. During the 1950s, Carl Jung recognized that music dealt with deep archetypal material and felt that it should be part of his work with each patient. Music motivates people to hate or to love, and it has curative powers. Larry Dossey, M.D., documented cases showing this fact in his book, *The Extraordinary Healing Power of Ordinary Things*.

Music has been used therapeutically with premature infants in many NICUs throughout the country. There are many online articles about music in neonatology, stating that there is evidence that music has beneficial effects when looking at both the behavioral and the physiological responses in a preemie. Not only has music helped relieve signs of agitation and distress, but it has been used to motivate preemies to learn to suck. It is also beneficial in relieving stress in parents of the babies.

In our NICU, music did not play over any speaker system. There were far too many tones and buzzers sounding from the myriad of medical equipment; these sounds were important for the nurses to hear and track. However, parents were told that they could play soft music in or near their infants isolette, and that this often soothed them when they were restless. My son and daughter-in-law did this a lot, and even today this grandson likes going to sleep with music playing.

Lullabies have been sung to infants from the beginning of time by mothers wishing to impart love to them or to soothe their restless bodies. Any new mother or father can tell you that their infant recognizes their voice and responds to it, so combining the familiar voice and harmonious notes may have a doubly positive effect. The staff in most NICUs encourage parents to talk to their child often and to sing to them, as well as play music for them. Kangaroo Care, when a parent holds the preemie next to his or her bare skin for an extended period, can be extra beneficial and comforting if soothing music is part of it. Humming has as good an effect as singing softly and perhaps is better than playing music. The sonic vibrations of the parent's voice comfort the infant while easing the parent's stress level. Many scientific reports highlight how humming or chanting have brought about positive changes in distressed or depressed patients.

My son heard right away how important Kangaroo Care was to a preemie and adjusted his life drastically so he could be a part of it while his baby was in the hospital. It caused financial hardship for them, but neither he or his wife, nor my husband and I, have ever questioned the wisdom of this decision. There are things that are more important than money. He could talk and hum to his son during this skin-to-skin contact on an every-other-day basis. It has made him a much different father than he would have been otherwise. He has a depth of connection to his son that few men have, because they have not had an opportunity to experience this sort of closeness before their child reaches normal birth weight.

Sound and music so influence us that they can help restore regular function of a body that is out of tune. Sound helps bring body, mind, and spirit into alignment. I have always loved music and found some of it deeply moving on a spiritual level. In grade school, I was part of a small choir that sang during daily Mass, and I still love to sing in church. I find singing an extremely meaningful kind of prayer because it involves my body and not just my mind. "To sing is to pray twice" is an old adage that holds profound truth.

I love liturgical music, both instrumental and vocal. During my twenty years of church work, I was lucky to be able to immerse myself in this. Latin chants still soothe, inspire, and uplift me as do many traditional and newly written hymns. Throughout my life, I have favored a wide variety of favorite popular artists and a few different styles, as do many people. Of course, poignant spiritual music can also often be found in popular music, such as the compositions of John Denver.

Many songs of John Denver have had a long-lasting and meaningful place in my life. Other people have told me that they, too, have been deeply touched by his music. In his book, *Seeking Grace in Every Step*, Catholic priest Mark G. Boyer talks of the force that inspired Denver's spirit and claims that spirituality is simply seeking grace. I caught some of this grace, while my grandson was in the NICU, through Denver's song entitled "For Baby (For Bobbie)" from his album *Rocky Mountain High* (see Appendix B). Its words reverberated through my spirit while I was thinking of what was happening in the NICU. Though written for a different reason, this piece of music—or its lyrics read as poetry—can accurately express a new parent's love and feelings. This simply shows the universal power of music and poetry.

A great way to nourish your own spirit with hopefulness is through deep listening. A marvelous album for this is *Songs in the Key of Hope* by Tom Jacobs. It overflows with a dozen inspirational songs that express the many faces of hope in our world that are sure to feed the listener's soul. When coupled with Tom's amazing voice, this CD is ideal to play while walking for exercise, strolling through a park, or driving back and forth to the hospital.

In his book, *Sounds of Healing*, Mitchell L. Gaynor, M.D., describes the various benefits of playing music in NICUs. He affirms that infants who were sung to or spoken to regularly showed weight gain and improved digestion. Lullabies and children's songs, as well as the spoken words of parents, have proven to work beneficially for the infant in many ways.

There's a lovely musical mantra that parents might want to use in Kathy Sherman's album, *The Heart Knows*; the mantra is titled the same. Several simple phrases mixed with beautiful, calming music make this piece ideal for use in the NICU. Listening to music can affirm the parent then soothe, as shown in this portion of lyrics from *Sometimes* in this same album.

> *Sometimes my tears just need a place where they can fall;*
> *A place that's safe where I can weep or sing or sigh;*
> *A place that lets me wonder why and silence never means, "Don't cry,"*
> *A place where tears can quench a thirsty soul.*

When my story needs a place of welcoming;
I know where I can go to speak the truth...

Many wonderful albums of lullabies are available to play for your child, and there are some music suggestions in the bibliography of this book. However, different people like different types of music. If blues, jazz, classical, country, or rock is more to your taste, that is where you should go to find music that feeds your adult spirit.

Since I am a poetry lover, I know well the power of poetry read aloud. Quality poetry is built on speech rhythms that create a certain melody to the ear that hears it read. If you've never liked poetry, perhaps looking at it from a new perspective will reveal unexpected depths. Have you ever considered that the reader can turn a simple poem into a form of prayer? Poetry, even not specifically sacred poetry, opens a window into the mystery of existence itself. Much like great music, genuine poetry touches us on deep, internal levels. It has the ability to uplift our spirits and to change and redirect our thoughts and hearts. Many poems hold a timeless truth beneath the surface of the words and can awaken the deep engines of our souls.

I read Lisel Mueller's poem, entitled *Hope*, often during the months my son and daughter-in-law were in Denver and included it in my photo-memorabilia album. To the last line of this poem I added, *and hope is in the NICU so far away*. Recently I discovered Mary Oliver's poem, *William*. Our baby had been named William Michael, so this poem quickly became a welcome addition to my long list of favorites. These poems and others are in Appendix B, and poems are easily found online.

Your child will also benefit from hearing whimsical children's poetry, even at this very early age. You might read your favorite love poem aloud to your baby or one from the back of this book. What is heard by the baby will be the soothing, calming comfort of your loving voice. What stirs within you will be deep meaning and connection that uplifts and sustains your spirit.

If you are an amateur artist who enjoys painting or sketching, this is a natural time to use your gift to express what is happening in your life. If a particular art form is your interest or passion, take time to visit a museum where you can surround yourself with your favorite art. Time spent this way may bring about a more hope-filled attitude. If the happiest days of your life have been spent on the ski slopes, and the season is right, take a day off now and then to ski. My son did this a few times. He has been an avid skier since junior high school and spent a few years living near and racing on the slopes following college. The bottom line is to care for yourself as well as the doctors and nurses are caring for your child.

NATURE

Nature is the art of God.
—THOMAS BROWNE, *Religio Medici* (1635)

All is born of water; all is sustained by water.
—GOETHE

People have a fundamental connection with nature and the plant world that is psycho-spiritual. Our connection to water and plants is as real as our connection to the air we breathe. How often do we pause to honor this great truth or let the goodness of nature permeate our spirits?

People who live in rural areas seem to have an easier time relating to nature than those who live in cities. Their experience seems to be one of conscious, daily communion, as evidenced by the works of so many poets and writers through the centuries. City dwellers have a different sort of experience of nature. They are not immersed in it, but they may respond to it when they have the opportunity. The recent resurgence of big city cooperative and backyard gardens speaks to the rising awareness that our relationship with the earth and its plants is important. This connection is a good thing for many reasons.

Deep within us lies a certain synchronicity with nature that has an emotional effect on us. For example, we are more reflective when we awaken in the darkness of night or when the fog rolls in. The cultivation of an appreciation of nature will enhance our own spiritual life. NICU parents might want to focus on nature to better care for their own spirits during this critical time and consciously try to hear and see nature speaking a new language to them. Most big cities have beautiful, large, well-maintained parks and city forests with huge old trees or lovely and delightful botanic gardens in which to walk and enjoy the beauty of nature.

Further, many plants and herbs have medicinal qualities. For thousands of years, the most effective medicines the world had available were made from plants, so it is well documented that plants do have a great healing power. Plants not only heal physical ailments but also foster emotional healing. And simply viewing or smelling a beautiful plant or surrounding oneself with nature can bring a sense of peace. The World Health Organization says that 80 percent of the planet's population still relies upon traditional plant-based medicine. Products that are good for stress reduction are available at any natural health food store and can be researched on the Internet.

Mary Oliver, who is one of my favorite poets, expounds upon the power of beauty in nature in her poem, "Where Does the Temple Begin, Where Does It End?" Many of her other poems deal directly with nature. Oliver and other poets sense sacredness in nature and express it in myriad ways. Certain cultures draw heavily upon the natural world. For instance, Native Americans use pollen in their religious ceremonies, summoning the participants to greater health. For some people, this same sort of connection can be found with animals. If you're one of these people, perhaps an afternoon at the zoo would provide a pleasant yet soothing and healing respite from the NICU routine.

A reawakening to the music that water provides can add a fresh and meaningful depth to any person's life perspective. Water features, or small fountains emitting soothing sounds, are often found now in medical waiting rooms, as well in churches and spas. This practice speaks subtly to the healing, calming, and nourishing power of water. The rushing and gurgling sounds of rivers, streams, and creeks are also very soothing. Moving water calls us to delve deep inside ourselves. It washes away, whether by ripple or wave, the shocks of the day that have visited our souls.

Beginning in my Girl Scout years and continuing today, my favorite place to hike is a trail that runs alongside a creek or a stream. I greatly enjoy the variety of musical sounds that are nature's auditory gift on such treks. Some rivers have a mystique all their own, giving off a musical, rambunctious sound—a kind of a metronome of the spirit, fluidly rolling and churning away worries or stresses. Waterfalls hold a particular fascination for me also. Perhaps it's the Celt in me, but I imagine ancient peoples trying to draw forth from their crude instruments sounds duplicating what they would hear in the water flowing over rocks, running downhill around bends, and cascading over ledges. My husband and I camp along the Rio Grande River each summer, sitting together to watch the river tumble and swirl around rocks and boulders each evening—he after hours of fishing, me after short hikes or hours of reading by its side. For me, it's a time when burdensome perceptions are cleansed and I am filled with a calm, Greater Awareness. The rise and fall of my breath connects with the rhythmic ebb and flow of the water, letting the river work its cleansing magic on my spirit.

One of our favorite hikes in this area is about seventeen miles south of Creede, Colorado, in the Weminuche Wilderness. The Ivy Trail slowly rises through thick forestation and follows a small stream that musically plunges and surges over ledges and around bends. Sometimes I stop and soak my feet in a pool of quiet water and watch the the music created upstream and downstream. Variations of this music happen all along the trail, on the walk up and the walk down. It is a most relaxing and refreshing way to spend a few hours on a warm afternoon, and it fills my spirit well.

In addition to the music that comes from the moving, falling waters, songbirds provide more wonderful music in nature. When you listen to the lilt and flow of the music of birds, you can almost feel their inner spirits rising and lifting with each note. Those notes can become symbolic of small lifts and improvements in the little life back in the NICU.

Nature provides music to the eyes as well as to the ears. Be conscious of everything around you. Let your spirit flow through all your senses as you take a walk in a park. Enjoy the chattering of a squirrel as it warns you away from its young and the cawing of crows as they catch air currents and engage in their graceful and rambunctious play. At sunset, view the gift of low-flying clouds as they become lit from behind, changing from red to purple to a glowing soft pink. Stop and view a beautiful flower or a bush ablaze with blossoms in a garden. Simply sit still for a period of time under a shade tree and drink in the reality that the tree might have something to say to you. Be still like me; be still, be still. Let God speak within you and your anxious thoughts will grow silent.

While walking or sitting still, you can take a mental vacation. Imagine a favorite relaxing vacation place with good fresh mountain air or a sea breeze; picture yourself there and enjoying every moment. Or imagine smelling the ripening fruit in warm sunshine while you're picking it in a country orchard to make your own home-baked pie or jam. Or remember a time in your past when you were able to spend a satisfying morning in your own flower garden, planting bedding plants that were going to provide a summer's worth of color and pleasure. Be good to yourself and open yourself to the seductive power of nature and all of the good gifts that it provides.

The natural world is a great gift and sometimes helps us escape real life and come back a better person. While nature is important, our relationship to family and friends, and our interaction to people as a whole, is much more vital to our well-being.

COMMUNITY

Let there be no purpose in friendship save the deepening of the spirit.
—KAHLIL GIBRAN

ommunity support helps people emotionally, especially when they are dealing with serious issues. In "Healing and the Community," a chapter in Bill Moyers' *Healing and the Mind,* Dr. David Smith highlights the importance of community in the healing process. Though he is speaking mostly about the medical and the neighborhood communities, at one point he does stress that most often, to find relief from stress, people turn to friends, family, and religion. Studies consistently show that more and better social support from family and friends is associated with positive outcomes in a patient's life. Feeling supported by others may serve as a buffer that reduces stress hormones during traumatic situations. Moreover, social support positively affects the cells that make up the body's immune defenses. Simply by being present, friends or family members may unknowingly shield the parents from the consequences of stress—and, often, the more friends the better. They are the natural backup to the wonderful medical community that is so professionally supporting preemie parents.

It is amazing, yet dependably true, that in times of hardship, people respond generously. People want to help out to show that they care; they hope their actions will improve a difficult situation. Those suffering hardship will say over and over again that it was the concern and well wishes expressed by friends and strangers alike that helped to uphold them enough to get through the next hour, the next day. The birth of a premature infant puts parents in the situation to be on the receiving end of thoughtfulness. Receiving is uncomfortable for many people, as expressed in the old saying, "It is easier to give than to receive."

Graciously receiving attention and consideration from others is a mutually beneficial experience. Friends and family members feel helpless and want desperately to be able to do something to help out the new parents. Here are some suggestions. One good place to start is with any older children in the family who need child care. An offer to bring the older child to visit the hospital might be well received at certain times. If you are bringing a sibling to visit, be sure to give him or her a small present or treat. You might also assemble a care package for the parents containing things such as gum, lifesavers, pain relievers, Tums, and Pepto-Bismol to temporarily relieve symptoms of stress. A lovely journal in which to record the passage of days would be a nice gift, or maybe a pedometer to track their exercise. Each act of kindness and assistance is unique to the giver, and hopefully the wishes of the new parents will be taken into consideration as the days move on.

Communication is important and often has to take place at odd moments of the early morning or evening because of differences in schedules on both sides. E-mail, certain websites, or a blog are great ways to keep many folks informed of the ups and downs of the journey. Current technology allows instant contact, so setting up a group e-mail address with everyone the new parents wish to inform of the baby's progress (or who has asked to be informed—with the parents' approval) would be another considerate gift to parents.

Perhaps one of the greatest gifts that could be given to a mother or father of a preemie is therapeutic touch, a healing modality thought to reduce pain and aid relaxation. Consider a gift certificate for a massage for either parent or for a facial and spa time—or a new hairdo—for Mom. A gift card to a nearby exercise center would probably be welcomed. The tried and true methods of visits, cards, flowers, and similar offerings are good but must be adapted to accommodate life in the NICU. For example, too many flowers don't work well in intensive care units; some hospitals don't allow them. Visitation policy varies from hospital to hospital.

Keep in mind that humans aren't the only source of healing support and friendship available. Interaction with animals can be therapeutic for animal lovers, too. Pets have a calming influence and may actually lower blood pressure by simply offering companionship and affection. If the parents have a pet they have not been able to give much attention to since the birth of their child, knowing that you are giving their animal its daily exercise will calm their concerns. Or better yet, you could meet them outside the hospital with their pet once or twice a week so they could walk it in the park themselves, while getting in their own exercise.

There are times the parents may seem so distracted and disconnected that you question whether what you want to do will make a difference. Rest assured that if you are a friend or family member of parents with a child in a NICU, anything you do will be important support to them. Any act made with good intention holds positive potential, but it might not hurt to check with one of the nursing staff or spiritual caregivers before taking action if you have concerns. Community support is one of the most vital and meaningful things that carries families through the birth and aftermath of caring for a premature child.

While my son and daughter-in-law were in Denver, they received countless visits from family and friends. Our oldest son—who is very busy because, among other things, he is the father of a very large family—made several visits, a couple of times bringing along some of the rest of his family. In addition to uncles and aunts of the new baby, both sets of grandparents visited when able and, blessedly, a great grandmother on my daughter-in-law's side was able to make the trip to visit. Many college friends of my son and daughter-in-law's reconnected, and lots of people from Montrose made sure to visit when they were in the Denver area for whatever reason. Some brought handmade gifts and others delivered artwork from the schoolchildren my daughter-in-law left behind. Since visits to the NICU are limited, it was only family who were able to see the baby briefly. But that was alright, because these friends knew how vital it was to show the parents some care and compassion. It is hard to say how important these visits were; my feeling is they were invaluable, and my children agree.

RITUAL AND THE PREEMIE FAMILY

At best, reading about ritual will stimulate your mind; actually doing it, on the other hand, will stimulate your life.
—KATHLEEN WALL AND GARY FERGUSON

People like ritual. Whether we acknowledge it or not, we are surrounded by ceremony and ritual from the time we are young, and we find deeper meaning in life by participating in it. Actions and events such as handshakes, hugs, bows, gift-giving, parades, birthday parties, and the opening ceremonies at sporting events are all familiar rituals, interactions that give us the ability to send and receive messages. Most of us find such things important; ritual is a fundamental form of human communication.

When it comes to expressing religious beliefs or communicating with God, some people find the word "ritual" worrisome or see it as a negative. If this is the case for you, might it be time to look at it through the eyes of experts on the subject? For others who are more comfortable with expressing their beliefs through ceremony, this might be an opportunity to expand their perspective and see new possibilities.

Angeles Arrien, author of *The Four-Fold Way*, says that ritual is recognizing a life change and then doing something to support the change and honor it. The birth of a premature child brings about a dramatic change in family life. When we meaningfully join in, or conduct, a ceremony, we are embracing our own power in this life change. We make sense of things as they are and approach life in a healthy, holistic manner.

Sometimes, because of worry or anxiety and trying to balance job and other family interactions, parents of the preemie may feel a sense of emotional or spiritual paralysis. They may feel extremely tired and somewhat lost. They find their emotions on a roller-coaster ride and may even experience physical illness. Larry Dossey, M.D., in *Recovering the Soul*, reminds us that an image of one person can affect the physiology of another. With all that medical science tells us today about the connection between mind and body, there is no reason to think that ritual would not help enhance the immune system and have a positive physical effect. Taking part in a ritual allows your mind to expand and your spirit to rise and changes your mood, according to Barbara Biziou, an expert on practical spirituality.

Ordinary life can become extraordinary when one engages in meaningful ceremony, and extraordinary happenings will be honored properly. Rabbi Harold Kushner, author of the international bestseller *When Bad Things Happen to Good People*, talks about the value of ritual while explaining an aspect of the Jewish religion. He states that ritual is soul activity, nourishing everything about us that is not physical—our thoughts, our values, our memories, our future actions, or the choices we will make.

According to Jon Kabot-Zinn, Ph.D., who founded the Stress Reduction Clinic at the University of Massachusetts Medical Center, soul is wrapped up with a sense of the heart being touched by feelings. "Soul" has to do with a person's journey, seen as a story that has a much deeper inner meaning. A premature child's birth is certainly an open doorway into the domain of the soul, and part of soul work is to honor the pain. The grief and fears of the parents need to be held tenderly and honored in the same way that joy and happiness over a healthy, full-term baby would be.

Melody Beattie, a bestselling author and a popular speaker, has made her lifetime work helping people deal with difficult problems in order to transform their lives because of them. She believes that low moments can be made into magical moments that become the turning points of our journey. The answer to what we need to do next lies deep within us, and an activity such as a ritual may be just the thing to prompt that answer.

Elisabeth Kubler-Ross, M.D., a pioneer in the field of death and dying and a person who worked with very ill children, tells us that many times she witnessed a wonderful experience growing out of a disaster. Whereas the medical team supports the family as they care for their child, family and friends provide essential emotional support. Ritual gives an opportunity to respectfully and gratefully include and honor these special people, while stirring the spiritual depths of all who take part.

Matthew Fox, Ph.D., an Episcopal priest and founder of The Institute in Culture and Creation Spirituality, believes that being involved with community and with ritual are wonderful ways to nourish the soul. He feels that one of our problems as a people is that we lack common rituals or we choose not to involve ourselves in them when the opportunity arises. It doesn't matter whether parents and family of the preemie are connected with a particular religion or whether they consider themselves spiritually alive. Even if they live their life from an unbeliever's approach, taking part in a ceremony can be very meaningful. Marianne Williamson, who has lectured and written on spirituality and metaphysics for over twenty-five years, tells us that people want rituals to be not fancy, but genuine. We do not need a written ceremony so much as we need authenticity before God; we do not need an ordained person to perform our ritual as much as we need to have spirit-filled consciousness and internal simplicity. Especially in a secular, fragmented society such as ours, personal ritual can be a powerful, practical way to capture or ease emotional energy.

The birth of a premature child and its growth are unique experiences in life. They offer a seldom-recognized invitation to conduct a ritual, and any time during the first weeks or months of the child's life would be an appropriate time for this to happen. A ceremony may help give a sense of resolve, comfort, hope, and direction, or it may be an expression of joy.

During the few days I was near and in the NICU following my grandson's birth, I was hoping that the ritual of baptism would be a sustaining force. Since it was not for my children, and only spoke to me in a very limited way, I began thinking of another opportunity to have a ceremony. I knew the new parents had a very skilled, caring community supporting them at the hospital, a mountain range away from home, but I was aware that there would be hard times for this new family once the baby was released from the hospital. It seemed to make sense to look toward a time when they were settled in at home and had established some kind of normal routine. I began collecting pieces of music, scripture, and things that would be appropriate symbols. A welcome home ceremony easily came together. A few weeks after they were home, I surprised them with the idea; I soon learned it would have been better to include them in the planning. Following is a ritual for both adults and children; it includes an activity with dollar bills that will delight and teach the children. It can be a model for others; the complete ceremony appears in Appendix A.

Someone who has never done this before might ask exactly how does one put a ritual together? How can something new and foreign be incorporated into busy, stressful times? Meaningful ceremony does not have to be complicated, and it can be formulated according to the belief of those gathered. There are just a few things to be aware of in order to create a solid, expressive ceremony. The recipe for a meaningful ritual has six key ingredients:

Intention—reason or purpose

Sequence—beginning, middle, ending

Dedicated space—an outside area such as a private garden; inside private room, such as around a dining table or in a comfortable living room. Whatever area is used, create a unique focus, perhaps with a draped, colored cloth and special seating arrangement.

Objects—lighting, flowers, candles, music, symbolic objects, readings

Personal meaning—signifying something in your heart that will reach others

Leader—someone to begin and end the experience, as well as cue other participants

Sarah York, who has a Master of Divinity degree from Harvard Divinity School, encourages the use of music and readings that nourish the soul, ground the spirit, and invite emotional release. They are not essential to the structure of the service, but they offer spiritual nourishment and touch universal chords of human feeling. If you use them, choose them carefully; be aware of being as inclusive as possible of the various perspectives of people in attendance.

Music provides a healing effect. Chosen music may be secular or religious; choose any style you like personally. Use music once, or at most twice, during the ceremony. It may just be a quiet, reflective piece following a reading.

Readings come in many forms. You can use anything from a child's storybook to scripture, to poetry, to something written especially for the occasion. The selections should be intentional and used sparingly.

If a cloth is used in the environment, give some thought to which color would hold deepest meaning. For example, blue might be the grandmother's and namesake's favorite color, or green could be a symbol of spring, when the child was born. Symbolic objects are limitless; a few examples are leaves, shells, rocks, chimes, pictures, magazine cutouts, candles, icons, crosses, or other religious symbols.

Before beginning a ceremony, talk to those who attend, explaining briefly the content or structure; keep it simple and clear. It will help participants focus on the ritual itself and allow them to join in at a deeper level. Remember that location will affect the quality of the experience: turn off phones and fax machines; place a "Do Not Disturb" sign on the doorbell or door to the room.

Background music may be played as people arrive. A simple act such as removal of shoes, asking participants to quiet themselves, the washing of hands with scented water, the sprinkling of water, or the lighting of a candle will signify the beginning of the ritual. At the ending, blow out the candle and thank the people for coming.

There is within each of us an untapped source of peace, wisdom, and guidance. Ritual allows us to slow down, quiet our minds, tune in to our bodies, and allow the creative juices to flow.

Parents may feel too overwhelmed and busy to create their own ceremony while the baby's life is very fragile. Friends and family members are eager to do something helpful and might want to help create a ritual. However, it is essential to obtain the parents' permission to do so and to involve them in the planning if they wish to be. Ceremonies or formal prayer experiences might be helpful at different times. Here are some suggestions for rituals appropriate for a premature birth.

Soon after delivery is a sacred time for parents; some might wish to keep the time private, but others might want to raise it to a more sanctified level by inviting a formal blessing time by a chaplain. Some people prefer to wait until a few days after the baby is born to have a solemn dedication, naming, or baptism ceremony.

When parents are feeling anxious or afraid, a planned ritual or prayer time can help relieve some of their worries. One good time for a ritual is if the infant must have surgery. A ceremony at that time lets parents formally acknowledge their belief system, for example, by entrusting their child to the Creator. A ritual can also recognize concern about the parents' financial well-being because of long periods away from the job or future financial burdens because of the long hospital stay.

Most hospitals have a formal gathering when it is almost time for the baby to leave for home, giving the parents and all the medical caregivers a chance to celebrate the leave-taking. Our children had a wonderful going-away party; more is said about that in the stories in Part Two. If your hospital does not do this, arrange a time when at least a few of the caregivers can get together with you and a few family members or close friends to honor the occasion.

The baby's homecoming gathering is an ideal occasion for a ceremony involving the extended family and friends. An organized ceremony is an important time to come together to give thanks and celebrate on a much deeper and more spiritual level than a traditional baby shower could achieve. One suggestion is to allow the new parents and baby time to acclimate to being a family on its own for a few weeks. Without the ever-present medical help that they are used to, it will take time to allay anxiety and hyper-vigilance about the baby's well-being

Some rituals—for example, a naming ceremony—are usually conducted by a hospital chaplain or the family's minister or rabbi. However, a family member or close friend who knows the parents better than a chaplain does might be a better person to create and lead this ritual or others. These ceremonies can be short or a bit longer—whatever is needed to address specific needs. Rituals are easily tailored to fit any ethnic background, faith perspective, belief system, or personal experience. Perhaps only one or two of these ceremonies will seem appropriate for certain parents. What is done will vary with the situation and desires of each couple.

Consider how such occasions can help honor all you have been through, letting you tell this particular portion of your unique life story. Keep in mind that our spirituality is expressed as only we can express it—by our attitudes, our behavior, our bodily expressions, and our life choices, and in what we deny or what we affirm.

PART TWO:

The Sharing of Stories

If stories come to you, care for them.
And learn to give them away where they are needed.
Sometimes a person needs a story more than food to stay alive.
—BARRY HOLSTUN LOPEZ

Story Empowers and Transforms

Most new mothers immediately begin telling people what it was like following a birth experience. You'll struggle to express the depth of emotion and the reality of experience that has permeated every moment of your life these past few hours. For both of the preemie's parents, it is especially important to tell of these happenings and to express what has become of all your dreams surrounding this new child. Likewise, it is necessary for those who love you to hear your thoughts and feelings.

Each of us has struggles, beliefs, opinions, blind spots, and points of view. People express themselves differently and have brain patterns and verbal responses that happen often without much thought and reflection. Some people are more introspective and less demonstrative than others, but one truth affects us all: we all live with stories—stories of others that we hear and stories of our own that we tell. These not only empower us, but also our future lives.

In civilizations around the world, storytellers are respected and honored because they express and preserve the culture and history of society through their stories. Religions have depended on story to express moral values and guidelines for thousands of years. Families shape their own identity through the telling of stories, as do the individuals within the families. Stories hold the quiet ability to strengthen and inspire and to move us to take positive action.

Stories are ripe with potential much like a fresh, juicy red apple. As we bite into the apple, it nourishes us with each bite. It speaks deeply to the senses of touch, smell, and taste. Similarly, each small seed has the potential to bring forth a new sturdy tree if planted in the proper soil and watered and pruned with care. And so it is with story when it makes its way through an open, fertile, and seeking human spirit. There's the possibility of inspiration because of understanding and connectedness through the common experience.

From the time I was a little girl, I have loved reading and hearing stories. I often spent hours on end lost in the lives and experiences of the characters in a book. Scripture stories came alive in my imagination. It was not until my college years, when I studied literature and poetry in earnest that I began to understand the universal power of story. As my studies continued much later in life with a focus on psychology, the healing power of story became a fascinating new perspective to integrate into my awareness. As any doctor or nurse will tell you, healing is a process, and I feel story can play an important role in that process.

In *The Spirituality of Imperfection*, Ernest Kurtz and Katherine Ketcham point out that stories convey the mystery and miracle of being alive. They remind us that storytelling itself gives no quick fixes but relays a gradual process that points to a time of healing. In story, we try on the insights and experiences of others, and whatever matches our own becomes significant, holding promise for the future.

It is hard to overemphasize the importance of story and storytelling in nurturing one's spirituality. When a person finds his or her life turned upside down, when expectations are shattered, it is natural to ask the question, "Why has this happened?" The medical community surrounding the worried parent will have good, concrete answers, but the question "Why" begs deeper examination, because we are not solely physical beings. We persist in asking why, especially when we are hurting and ache for normalcy. In times of trouble, people might turn to storytelling as a way of exploring the mystery of "why has this happened to me" and "what am I going to do about it." Stories remind us that life holds many hurts, but in the pain, and the journey out of it, is where our healing will begin.

Some questions may never be answered by others, but only by walking our personal path from hurt to healing. In the days and months after the birth of your baby, you will find yourself telling your story often to friends and family members. Doing so will release the events from the mental arena where they are played over and over again. With each telling will come an emptying out and a small sense of liberation.

Many people believe that telling a story about a difficult situation makes it possible to bear it. Stories can teach and inspire us; they carry wisdom that can help us sink deeper into our spirit and show us how to have faith and hope. Upon hearing a story from others who have experienced similar happenings, we often find inspiration to believe that our own growth and comfort will be possible. They show us how to become and change. Others' stories provide meaningful metaphor for those who hear them. Deep-seated thoughts and energies will be created within the mind and spirit of readers as they awaken to the profound connection they have with another person's story. With this in mind, our family members offer their own stories.

First is the mother's story, followed by the stories of the father, a grandmother, and then a grandfather. Because each family is unique and each person different, these stories will vary from what the reader is experiencing, yet there will be common threads that can provide hope and optimism. These stories also hold the potential to broaden understanding and closeness between the generations.

At the back of the book, the same story is told from the perspective of the premature child. It is a section for small children and adults alike. This story is a way to make a premature infant's days in the NICU more understandable and friendly in the eyes of a child. Perhaps siblings or cousins who live far away are unable to see the newly born child for many weeks. The substitute teacher who took over my daughter-in-law's classroom would have appreciated such a story to read to her second graders. Children will hear adults discussing what is happening in the hospital they cannot visit and will sense the anxiety and worry that accompanies the many unfamiliar words they hear. Their own fears may take on unrealistic proportions. Even if siblings are able to visit, this section might help familiarize them with what is happening with their new brother or sister and help them better understand why Mom and Dad are unable to be at home for long periods of time. They will be able to see the step-by-step progress of the child in the story and then compare it to their own new sibling. You, as parents, might use this story in the same way, as a gauge through which to view your own child's possible development. Most important, you will see that there is real hope for a good and happy outcome for you.

Some babies are born in nine months, by the clock.
Some babies are born, and they sit up and talk.
Some babies are born and no doctor is there.
But some babies come in on a wing and a prayer.
—GARRISON KEILLOR

See *Jeffery's Poem* p. 98

The Mother's Story

...birth is but a sleep and a forgetting;
The soul that rises with us, our life's star...
trailing clouds of glory do we come...
—WILLIAM WORDSWORTH

*T*he nurse brought me into the dimly lit room and I lay down as she checked my blood pressure, probably for the twentieth time in two months. I tried my best to relax, to take deep breaths, thinking about how my blood pressure hasn't been so great the last five prenatal visits. "Breathe," I told myself. The nurse left without saying anything. My doc came in a few minutes later. I knew it the minute he walked in: his face told it all. He said, "Carin, I'm so sorry, but I've just called over to the hospital and I want you to spend the night for a twenty-four hour observation." The tears streamed down my face. On my way out to the car, I called my husband, Barrett, and asked him to meet me at the hospital. Once I checked in, it was constant stress. There were phone calls to find a substitute for my classroom full of second graders and sub plans to make. Nurses and docs strapped wires and hoses to me and drew my blood as I made and took calls to and from family and friends. Ugh! My world just turned upside down.

Father Don came and prayed over me while administering a sacrament called "Anointing of the Sick." It was a ritual of prayer and healing, but it disturbed me because it was the first time I thought that I might not make it through this—or that my baby might not. That second thought was to haunt me over and over again in the weeks ahead. Would healing prayer be enough to get us both through what was going to be happening?

The next few days were a blur. First was my ob-gyn's diagnosis of preeclampsia, then careful observation and monitoring, coupled with his conversations with doctors in Denver. Finally, there was a decision to send me from our hometown in western Colorado over the mountains to Denver on the Flight for Life airplane. I can't thank my ob-gyn enough. He didn't want such a young baby to be born without the very best medical care available. Looking back, he saved both of our lives.

I struggled with the realization that I would leave my classroom and second graders, my home, my family, and my friends behind. My husband was such a caring, responsive warrior through all of this. Not only did he have to worry about his work, he also had to figure out plans for our dog and go back home and pack for me and himself. He came back to the hospital with my bag that consisted of one maternity outfit, the black Lab stuffed animal from the nursery, and something like thirteen pairs of underwear for me. He said, "I had a hard time thinking about what you'd need." Honestly, how were we supposed to pack? Was I going to be pregnant for the rest of the term or not? We didn't really want to think of me not being pregnant at twenty-five weeks gestation. I had barely come halfway! I remember Barrett's face on the plane ride and both ambulance rides...calm but tense. I felt fine. I didn't fully understand all this commotion.

The next few days were once again a blur. New doctors to meet and to be examined by—an ob-gyn, interns, residents. There was a multitude of medical technicians, nurses, friends, and family. More phone calls for more sub plans and questions about where I put that "thing" in my classroom that they needed. We arrived in Denver on a Friday and, on Monday night, Barrett finally decided to go spend the night at our friends' house. He had slept on a hospital chair for the past seven nights. I was happy that he had a place to go. That same night, after numerous antacid pills to try to get rid of my two-day heartburn, which I thought was from the adobo burrito I ingested on Saturday, the night nurse took a blood sample again. Ten minutes later she was back, checking my blood pressure and asking for another urine sample to check my kidney function. Another ten minutes went by and she was back with news that I was heading downstairs to be prepped for an emergency C-section. My liver and kidneys were failing, and I needed to get this baby out immediately. Could I ask my husband to get back here as soon as possible?

I called Barrett before I was taken downstairs. "You need to get back here, I'm having a baby!" He was there and in scrubs, ready to go, in forty minutes. A doc kept him busy with idle conversation in the hallway while I received a spinal tap. The nurses caring for me were gentle and professional, and I took comfort in knowing they had done this before. "Good!" I thought. The C-section started at 12:43 a.m. and William Michael Beshoar was born at 12:55 a.m., December 14—almost exactly three months early. I remember my body shaking from the anesthesia during the whole surgery; luckily, Barrett held my hand the whole time.

Our 830-gram (1 lb. 13 oz.) baby boy had a Christmas cap on his tiny head when I got to see him for the first time. They held him up in front of me for a brief kiss to his forehead, then he was taken off to receive his own emergency medical care. The next time I saw him was the following day at four a.m., a full twenty-eight hours after he was born, when I left post-op and was rolled back to my room upstairs. I was on a gurney, still a little foggy, but so grateful to see my baby boy. My arms ached to hold him, but that would not happen for a while.

Lots of sleep and more docs, nurses, family, and friends followed during the next few days. Again, it was Barrett the Brave in charge. He was the strong, level-headed husband, father, son, and brother—and now liaison to all things medical. I got to visit Liam several more times the day after I first entered the NICU: me in a wheelchair with Barrett navigating the elevator and hallways down to the sterile, dimly lit nursery.

Ah, the NICU. I thought, "Why is it that so many dimly lit places are meant to calm but generally are places of high stress?" The NICU, our home away from home for nearly four months, was Liam's first home. Upon entering, I was impressed by the careful hand washing and sterilizing before entering the babies' area. So much careful hand washing was necessary before entering the sterile land of buzzers and alarms. It was to become for me a multilayered land of stress, despair, fear, tears, questioning, trust, nurturing, comfort, hope, growth, knowledge, milestones, smiles, laughter, security, friendships, peacefulness, and healing. I soon felt like a medical student when I left the NICU each day. Our nurses were what made the NICU survivable. Christine and Judy, our primary day nurses, were also our counselors, medical experts, nannies, and educators—always there with a shoulder to cry on or a hug in celebration.

My body began to heal as soon as they sewed me together. My blood pressure remained a problem for a while. The day after I was discharged, I had to come back to the emergency room and spend another night in the hospital until new medication began working and there were signs of lowered pressure. My milk came in fast and plentiful and the nurses instructed me in the love/hate art of breast milk pumping. My breasts were transformed into these massive, heavy, unrecognizable appendages that were vital nourishment for the very tiny boy downstairs. From that day forward, pumping occurred every three hours for the next four months without fail. New purchases came next—a breast pump, bras, clothes, and baby blankets. The stuffed black Lab dog from our nursery back home became a mascot who kept watch in or near the isolette, 24/7.

I got to change Liam's diaper and take his temperature for the first time four days after he was born. The same day, I got to hold him against me for the first time; they call it "Kangaroo Care." Eventually both Barrett and I learned to relax during Kangaroo Care, even with my stunned and loving parent paparazzi hovering. How could I blame them? The birth was momentous and long-awaited. I had to plan to wear clothes that would work well for Kangaroo Care. A zipper-front sweatshirt seemed best. I removed all clothing underneath, and then my tiny baby was placed on my bare chest with his bare body up against mine: finally, something that helped me connect with my child! If I could just stay like that every day, all day, I would have. We would sync our breathing rhythm and he would lay his head right under my chin. Kangaroo Care—love it! I could smell him on me even after I left the hospital and I didn't want to wash the smell away. I never knew when the next time would be, and God forbid if it never came again.

We became used to the fact that two good days in a row didn't occur very often, and so many days were a struggle. Liam needed to gain weight; he had dropped down to 767 grams. He needed a blood transfusion. He needed to breathe, and he kept having apnea episodes. He was on and off the ventilator repeatedly. We were constantly worried and fretful. It often seemed that the only positive thing in our day was that he was in the hands of very committed, knowledgeable, and caring docs and nurses.

Christmas was pretty difficult. It was the first real scare for me. Barrett and I spent Christmas morning opening a few gifts from family and my coworkers. We were eager to see Liam. When we got to the NICU, it had a much more somber feel that day. Liam's isolette had a screen around it and the lights were even dimmer than usual. The docs and nurses were there by our side as soon as we walked up. They knew to calm our fears immediately and quickly explained the changes. He was on a new ventilator that hummed, vibrated, and shook him slightly so his lungs never actually deflated. Several times throughout the previous night, he had stopped breathing, and it took them one to two minutes to "bring him back." This was a solution? Ugh!

We drove the ninety miles to my parents' house for dinner after that. Tears streamed down my cheeks the whole time we drove and reappeared often through dinner. We both were somber and distracted. My parents shared our mood and were supportive, concerned listeners. We stopped again at the hospital on our way back, and for the first time, I thought the worst: my heart jumped out of my chest because his isolette was gone! We were washing our hands and looking over at the space where he used to be. The look we gave each other was pure, unadulterated agony. The nurse was by our side as we dried our hands and quickly explained that they had moved Liam to an enclosed room so it would be quieter for him. He needed less stimulation to calm his agitations. His tiny little nose and mouth looked all disjointed with this new ventilator, and I couldn't kiss him. We both kissed our fingers and touched him. It was really hard to see Barrett, the dependable rock, visibly scared. He was the one who usually put me at ease, but not now.

The next day was better...thankfully. Routine life in the NICU went on. X-rays, periods of oxygen desaturation (d-satting), intubations, ultrasounds, steroids, use of continuous positive airway pressure (C-PAP), antibiotics, infections, and more blood transfusions continued to be an everyday occurrence for Liam. If it wasn't one thing, it was another. His lungs became the main source of conversation for a while. A positive constant was that he was gaining weight. I missed Liam when I wasn't there, but I was homesick as well. We had to stay sane, so we made sure to busy ourselves with friends and family when we weren't at the hospital. I would often just start crying or find tears welling up for no reason at all. Barrett wasn't sure how to deal with me when I got like that. We had several conversations about how we felt this situation could really pull a couple apart or bring them closer together; we both agreed that it was bringing us closer together.

There were some days, though, that really strained our relationship. Toward the end of January, I found it hard to keep my emotions in check, and I took it out on Barrett. A person can take only so much; I felt like I would explode if there was more bad news. We spent some time apart after cross words. I cried and felt so isolated, scared, and alone. I am so thankful that these times didn't happen too often. Ironically, the better Liam got, the more homesick I felt. I wanted to take my baby home and start living the life that I had been dreaming about for so long. Sometimes Barrett and I would go to a park, and I would see mothers with strollers and pregnant women. I looked enviously at new mothers and mothers-to-be. I never got to get big and round. I missed out on that.

Our family and friends really carried us through. It would have been an even harder battle to conquer without them. Some were regular: my parents, Barrett's parents, brothers, and sister-in-law. Our close friends were there for us, but they didn't visit the NICU often because they knew we were overwhelmed. Friends were what we needed. We house-sat for traveling friends part of the time; the rest of our time, we were at the Ronald McDonald House or at our friends Claire and Iain's home. We ate most of our meals at restaurants and the hospital cafeteria. We tried to find places to exercise as well: finding a good balance was important. All the while, I dutifully pumped breast milk every three hours. That was the one constant I could provide for myself and Liam.

We had Liam baptized early on, when he was about four days old—a little emotional and spiritual insurance...assurance. I prayed regularly and sometimes several times a day. There were so many people we knew, and a lot more we didn't know, who were praying for Liam the whole time. I believe to this day that the power of prayer carried him through—along with lots of medical science!

Every day, we grew a little more hopeful. He continued to grow and eventually he graduated into a regular crib. We were feeling more positive—but, alas, one more scare. It was the middle of February and he was now 2,040 grams (4 lbs. 8 oz.)!!! They had just weaned him off the C-PAP again and Barrett was holding him. Our regular nurse was not there that day. Actually, a nurse that we had never had before was his primary that day. Liam's oxygen level d-satted to below 40, he turned black, and stayed like that for what seemed like forever. We yelled for his nurse and we just didn't feel like she moved quickly enough. She eventually revived him and hooked his C-PAP back on. We were devastated. We had been so scared. We stayed a little while longer and made sure the doctor checked him out. Then we had to get out of there; it seemed as if we didn't leave the hospital, we would go insane. We took a cab to a favorite restaurant and ate and drank away our sorrows. I was so glad that we had each other and that we could help each other heal.

That was the last very negative experience we had. After that, it was a day-to-day battle to get him to eat by himself and breathe by himself.

It was a long process of constant vigilance, which was both emotionally draining and exhilarating. We had been there since December 10, and we got to take our boy home, up and over the mountains, on April 6. We had a list of instructions a mile long and an oxygen tank to accompany us on our trip. The ever-present stuffed black Lab rode in the back seat right next to Liam, who seemed swallowed up by his car seat. But it felt so good and exhilarating, and also a bit frightening, to finally be allowed to take our son home.

THE FATHER'S STORY

She's the one, the only remedy
Night nurse...
—GREGORY ISAACS

*H*er rounded, naked belly—barely twenty-five weeks pregnant—lay
exposed under the bright lights that reflected off of the polished stainless
steel surgical table. Scurrying nurses, anesthesiologists, and all their assis-
tants shrouded in green gowns, eyes covered with oversized shields and
clear glasses and their feet covered in ridiculous paper galoshes, rolled
tables of instruments into position; moves of their well-choreographed
dance were observed by another stationary wall of green tunics standing
rigid outside the intensity of the surgical floodlights. Their eyes were wide
and exposed. Some stared uncomfortably at me; one looked between the
bare legs of Carin, my wife, as she gazed at the ceiling, listening to the
instructions of the masked man who would bring her closer to death than
she had ever been.

The doctor noticed me eyeing the stationary imposters. "It's a teaching hospital," he said apologetically. "What's your name again?"

"Barr-ahhah...Barrett," I managed, clearing my throat.

"What line of work ya in?" He tried several more attempts at distract-
ing me. My wide eyes and cross brow were a dead giveaway. I was scared.
I've always been good at hiding what's going on in my head. A family
mask: something to be proud of and work on hard when you are young,
according to my grandfather. Not tonight.

"We're ready, Dr. Stephens!" an urgent voice shouted from the
other side of the table.

I found out over the next few days that Dr. Stephens was not gifted
in conversation. His small talk never improved from the first night we

met, before he carved the eight-inch incision in Carin's abdomen. He was never able to make eye contact for more than a moment, and he hurried his way through his thoughts, always making his point but leaving out details that left you wondering. He was one of those people whose thoughts moved faster than his mouth could ever hope to. His gifts resided outside the world of personal communication.

His kind eyes peered through horn-rimmed spectacles that were perched recklessly on a pronounced nose. Thick, dark hairs announced themselves proudly from both nostrils. Patches of salt and pepper whiskers hid in the folds of his tired, wrinkling face. A paunch protruded from his scrubs, more a product of stress and lifestyle than a lack of physical activity. Too many late nights at the hospital; I saw him at all hours. His responsibilities were enormous. He was the man in charge of interns, residents, and doctors from several departments of the hospital; he was also the key figure in monitoring my wife after the emergency C-section.

He was not imposing at first sight. It took five or ten seconds to realize he was a force; a kind, well-meaning ball of energy who kept the fires of St. Joseph's Hospital surgical staff burning with efficient passion. He burst into Carin's hospital room the next day, not waiting for the door to open enough for a clean entry. "Excuse me," he said to the room's occupants. "You can stay, Dad," he said, releasing the arms of his stethoscope to their resting place in his ears. My brother and mother turned to leave without comment, Mom squeezing my shoulder as she left.

He said to Carin, "Understand this: you and your baby were my patients last night, but *you* are my patient today. I want you taking it easy. He's in good hands." Five interns walked in carrying clipboards. Four blondes were dressed in bright colorful scrubs, most with hair pulled back in a functional ponytail, clipboards dangling from their long fingers. The lone brunette's scrubs were simple black, and she held her clipboard tightly to her chest as she silently followed the others into the room.

"Teaching hospital, you see..." He stopped to listen to whatever sounds came through the stethoscope. "Are you breastfeeding?" he asked Carin. "Good," he said without waiting for her response. "Let's see your nipples. Uhhh-huh. Uhhh-huh. Good," he said, closing her top back up. I caught a quick glance exchanged between two of the blonde interns, who certainly had been the envy of every girl in their high schools. I wondered what joke I was missing out on.

"I wish I could breastfeed," Dr. Stephens continued. "Breastfeeding's great! It's like forty-five minutes of high-impact aerobics everyday," he said. He enthusiastically swung his arms and marched in place. Everyone laughed except him. He left the room marching, "Huh-ha, huh-ha, huh-ha..."

"So, you've met Dr. Stephens," the tall blonde in pink continued her smile.

"Of course they have. He did their surgery last night," the brunette asserted as she stepped to Carin's side. "We have a few questions. I'm Nurse Winter. I was with you last night," she went on, pulling out her stethoscope and listening to Carin's heart one more time. She finished and read from her clipboard a list of questions that would become a familiar script over the next week while Carin recovered from kidney failure, a swollen liver, and extreme high blood pressure—all deadly symptoms of preeclampsia, a horrific side effect of pregnancy that lands thousands of families into the neonatal intensive care units, NICUs, of hospitals around the world.

A dull, gray fog was beginning to settle over me. Last night, after Carin's emergency C-section, I had walked with Liam and his army of doctors and nurses from the surgical center to the NICU. Taylor, who I later found out was a student finishing her RN degree, was assigned to me. I walked clumsily in my surgical garb. Her hand was in the small of my back, steadying me. The isolette rolled quickly down the hall with no one in particular pushing it. All eight armholes that gave access to its precious cargo were filled with purposeful, steady hands. Latex gloves wiped off the blood, pumped his too-young-to-function lungs with oxygen, took blood samples, and plunged a syringe that seemed as long as he was into his leg. The set of hands not holding life-saving instruments gently massaged his impossibly small torso.

When we reached the elevator, I registered my first clear glimpse of him. His ears were too big for a head that small. "Something that small shouldn't have ears," I thought. The reality was sinking in. At less than twenty-five weeks, his chances were slim.

"Easy baby...let me at you," the nurse holding the oxygen bag said. His penny- sized hands and pencil-thin arms batted at her, knocking the breathing apparatus away from his mouth. "He's strong," Taylor said, as a nurse placed the oxygen mask back over his mouth. I repeated these words to myself as I felt Taylor's hand return to my back. "He's strong."

Strong enough to beat the odds? Strong enough to be healthy? Strong enough to live?

The doors to the elevator opened and we made the sharp turn toward the NICU. Double doors opened and we rolled into the dark, cavernous intensive care unit. I was aware of faces watching us. Eyes switched from me to Liam, to me, and finally back to Liam. They rolled the isolette next to a glass-walled room marked "Surgery." I was aware of Taylor's hand on my back again and I turned to meet her eyes. She motioned me back toward the doors and I left his side for the first time.

"They will be very busy getting his new home hooked up for a few minutes. Let's get you changed," she said in an almost motherly tone. I looked down and saw blood smears on my chest. I continued looking at the blood-stained smock, holding it away from me, pinched between the thumb and index finger of each hand.

"From the birth. It's not his. From when you kissed him," she said, pulling off her mask and smock and throwing them into a hamper-like basket marked "Soiled Scrubs." I didn't remember kissing him. I was astounded. Taylor looked like she was sixteen years old; she was wearing Hello Kitty scrubs, of all things. She was not what I would have pictured if I had taken the time to do it.

She pulled off my cap and stepped around to untie my smock for me. I pulled my arms out of the sleeves and stood there, waiting to be told what to do next. I was completely receptive to any suggestion. I was standing inside the threshold of a world I knew absolutely nothing about. "Hello Kitty," I said softly. She threw my smock into the same basket.

"Not all boys fight like that," she said. Her hand purposefully moved up and her fingers ruffled my red hair. Looking back, it was an intimate, friend-like gesture. She felt sorry for me, and it wasn't just me that didn't know what to do or say. "It's a good sign," she said, smiling with her eyes but not with her mouth.

Her eyes went to my hair again. "Let me show you around. There are some things you'll need to know. You can spend as much time with him as you want," she said as she motioned me toward a sink prominently poised by the aisle of the NICU that was packed with rows of isolettes. "Your wife won't be missing you until tomorrow morning. She'll be pretty drugged up. Always remember to wash your hands."

The NICU was dark, but only because it was the middle of the night. I soon learned about the circadian rhythm. Sleep at night and rise and shine with the sun. As we stepped into the darkened aisle of isolettes, I was startled by the noise.

"Ding. Ding. Ding. Beep! Beep! Beep! Dooooht. Dooooht. Dooooht." Unfamiliar buzzers, bells, and alarms that controlled and monitored every facet of the babies' environments came from monitors that lingered with watchful eyes over each of the isolettes, Plexiglas table-sized incubators. The carpeted floors did little to stifle the sounds, but most of the babies slept. They looked much larger than Liam, I thought.

"These are the youngest babies in the unit," Taylor said. "We have twenty-two babies, twenty-three with your son," she corrected herself. As I walked down the aisle, Taylor told me about the rules of proximity. Parents and family were supposed to stay away from other babies: don't look, and certainly don't touch anything. "Steer clear of any activity," she said. "If the doctors or nurses are rushing, it's best to leave and give them space. You'll get used to the noises, and you'll know which ones are emergencies and which ones aren't," she continued.

We turned left through a large archway that opened to the middle aisle that was full of mostly empty isolettes. To my right was the glass room marked "Surgery," to the left was Liam squirming under the bright lights. Two people hovered over him now. I hoped they would be older than Taylor.

"Is this Dad?" asked a light-hearted voice. Plain green scrubs and masks covered him.

"Hi," I replied, sticking my hands in my pockets, hoping to avoid another introduction that I would never remember tomorrow.

"He's stable and should be through the night," he said. Those words hung in the air as I considered the possibilities of the meaning. "I'm Dr. Javier," he finished his introduction.

"It's day to day," the nurse said with concerned eyes peering over her mask. "I know you understand. He's very, very small." My mind reeled as I stepped to the side of the isolette and looked down at my son. He was no longer than my hand. Rolled-up white washcloths suspended his arms and lifted his legs under the knees, effectively holding them off of his sterile bedding. IVs came out of each arm and leg. Three metal leads were glued to his chest to monitor his breathing and his heartbeat. A tube that supplied oxygen to his limp body was taped with white surgical tape to the sides of his head. His eyes were emphatically closed, squinting under the bright surgical lights.

He was red and small and covered with wires. He looked more like a featherless baby bird than a boy. I looked closely at his diaper. It was the size of a quarter; "Pampers" was printed in baby blue across the front in tiny letters. I wondered to myself what font size the writing would be if it were word-processed. Four point? Six? I realized I was searching for scale. I was sizing him up, trying to comprehend how someone so small could possibly be alive. My mind was trying to quantify and measure the unquantifiable. I knew that I would have to tell my wife tomorrow. I needed definition to this strange and unexpected delivery.

"How much does he weigh?" I asked.

"It's not important," the doctor answered. "We'll be more concerned with the weight after a week. He's 830 grams, but he'll lose much of that over the next week or two." It all meant very little. He was small, smaller than I could imagine.

"Bong. Bong. Bong." The rhythm of the beeping from his monitors was hypnotic, each sound monitoring a vital sign. "Do you want to sit?" Taylor asked, motioning toward a large, well-worn wooden rocking chair. I gladly sat and looked around at the medical equipment that surrounded us. My eyes moved from high-tech gadgets to monitors to other equipment in the room. I heard Taylor's voice in my head, reminding me not to look at other babies and families. Several parents of other patients rocked in rocking chairs as they watched us. "Why are they all looking at us?" I thought.

The glass walls that separated the three aisles of the NICU were hardly visible, blocked by the hard, almond-colored cases that housed the most up-to-date—and incredibly expensive—equipment designed to save the lives of those who never would have lived as recently as five years ago. "The latest and greatest," we were told prior to Carin's surgery. I sighed, fought the building tears, and hoped it was enough.

I stood up and looked at Liam. He was struggling now; his arms and legs kicking at his cold new reality. The doctor and nurse were talking about medications. I looked at the tube that was taped to his head and went into his mouth. His lower jaw was clenching and chewing at it. I couldn't imagine the pain of being intubated. I looked at the large humming machine that was next to his isolette. It was obvious from the movement of two large synthetic bags enclosed in a plastic case that this was the machine that was helping him breathe. It made an awful, sucking sound as it urged air into the lungs of my son. "He's strong. He's strong."

I sat for several hours and watched him pull at his IVs and at his breathing tube. The longer I sat, the more detached I became. The room became fuzzy and nondescript. I hadn't slept, but the feeling wasn't exhaustion. I can describe it only as a disconnection between my spirit and my physical being. It was that dull, foggy feeling again; I would become intimate with it over the next several months.

The next two days are gone from my memory. I've rehearsed the events that I experienced many times over, trying to remember the details. All of the meetings: the priest who performed the baptism is nondescript; the social worker who helped us with paperwork might have been tall or short; the relatives and friends who met us in the hospital greeting room outside the NICU were many, but I couldn't name half of them. I was in shock, and I don't remember anyone telling me that I was. If I looked anything like I felt, how could they not notice?

Three days later, the fog began to temporarily recede. I was focused on watching Liam's weight. The nurses told us how much he weighed first thing in the morning on our visits. At 830 grams, he started out at almost two pounds; he now weighed 795 grams, and a slow downward spiral began that would not end for over seventeen days. Subsequent mornings brought a 5 to 10 gram loss.

Each day, I would walk through the double doors of the NICU and wash my hands. I was always greeted by the sounds of the monitors. My ear was trained after only a few days, and I had learned the difference between the good sounds and bad. Liam's lungs were too young to function. Even on the respirator—or C-PAP apparatus—he was still not receiving adequate oxygen, and his tiny body struggled through the pain of oxygen desaturation. I would approach his isolette and listen to the monitor. I hoped in silence for the slow rhythm of beeps that signaled, "Everything is OK, for the moment."

Christine and Judy were his primary day nurses. They were a contrast to each other in most every way, save their dedication to Liam. Christine, a short, rounded woman, had worked with preemies for over twenty years. She was a bundle of positive attitude that was always ready to make you laugh. She watched him during the day. Taylor, his night nurse and the young woman who had steadied and consoled me on the night of his birth, would now be responsible for his care. She was quiet, reserved, and competent. She lacked Christine's experience, but possessed the instinct and schooling to care for a medical emergency, or an emotional break-down of one of the NICU parents.

"He lost another 5 grams today," Christine mentioned with a smile. "We need to get this boy turned around." The heavy fog descended over me again, as it did every time there was bad news. I would lose myself in the smallest details, worrying about him losing more weight. I was obsessed with converting grams to ounces. How many more can he lose before he is a pound? The outside world was gone to me. I developed tunnel vision that could see only miniscule details through the thick haze that surrounded my spirit.

Carin was wheeled down in her hospital bed the day after her surgery, but left fairly quickly, feeling more in the way than anything. All the other patient's families watched us more closely when she was in the NICU in her giant hospital bed, or in the wheelchair that was the mode of transportation on a couple subsequent days. Carin would walk in tomorrow for the first time to sit with our son.

The next few days remained the same. Liam was still spiraling in the wrong direction: consistent weight loss, more constant oxygen desaturization, and now an inconsistent heartbeat were all the pattern of his early days in the NICU. His life was in a balance that was sickening to think about. One of his doctors finally told us to prepare for the worst. The honeymoon was over now; he was two weeks old, and he was showing no positive growth. There were struggles and experiences with death and revival.

He died for the first time on Christmas. His breathing stopped, and his heart stopped for what seemed like well over a minute. After the first few seconds, everyone stopped counting and started praying. Lifeless and still, he demanded the desperate attentions of a nurse too young and inexperienced to be put under this kind of pressure. A shot of adrenaline brought his body back to life. His first motion after the initial heartbeat was to swing his fists and kick with his wire-laden legs. A defiant slap at the reaper! Not tonight. Taylor was right. He was strong, but was he strong enough?

Taylor hugged us as we all cried. I remember feeling her body shake. A parent accepts this role in a world where anything can happen. Taylor willingly chose it as a profession; stresses and emotions that are unmanageable for most, she invited into her life. Labored lungs and gushing tears released the intense pressures of the past few minutes. It was relief, but for how long?

The next morning, we met another one of Liam's saviors. "Getting to know a preemie is a lot like getting to know a girl you want to date," Dr. Ben told me. He had been gone over the Christmas holiday and was just meeting us. He was a fit man with graying hair. He was either a young sixty or an exhausted thirty year old. I measured him up and decided he was the former. He spoke humbly, yet knowingly, about a baby whom he was just meeting. We would get to know Dr. Ben well over the next few weeks. He would work around the clock, making up for time taken over the holidays. The nurses seemed relieved that he was back, and there was a comfort in his confident demeanor.

The day after we met Dr. Ben, I walked into the NICU on a sleepless night and he was staring at Liam with a perplexed look on his face. As I washed my hands, I watched him. He didn't move until I finally had to approach, worried about his strange posture. "Hi, Dad. *Barrett*, isn't that an English name? This little lad is Irish. Look at his red hair."

The topic of conversation threw me, but it was welcome. "He's Irish—and Dutch," I answered. He sat down in the rocking chair with his legs spread wide, hands clasped behind his head. He was comfortable—at home.

Taylor walked up and beamed a smile. "Look!" she said handing me his chart. "He put on ten grams!" I didn't know how to respond. I felt like crying, but looking at the laid-back Dr. Ben and the grin on Taylor's face, it didn't seem right. Tears released from somewhere that I hadn't learned to control. Dr. Ben smiled, and Taylor looked me in the eye and softly said, "See, he *is* strong."

My mind was reeling, trying to figure out how much 578 grams was. Did he drop below a pound? Did it matter now that he had gained weight for the first time? I was trying to make sense of it all through the shroud around my head. I had been living inside this fog for so long that interacting with people was difficult. 578 grams. That's well above a pound—1 lb. 2 oz., actually. She was right. He *was* strong.

Over the next few weeks, we were rewarded with daily weight gains. We continued the all important Kangaroo Care, with the length of time together increasing as he grew. Liam would lie on our bare chests and sleep. The beats of a heart, the heat of our skin, and human touch had been taken from him, but we did our best to substitute. We gave him loving touches, as much as his frail frame would allow, but mostly we tried to let him sleep. Carin spent countless hours each day and night attached to a breast pump. I did my best to hold myself together in a strange city under stranger circumstances.

Liam spent nearly four months in the NICU. Clinically speaking, he died one more time when his lungs and heart gave us yet another wake-up call. He was revived and we were horrified. When would it all end? He was over four pounds and we were not expecting this type of setback. There was a trip for tests to another hospital, guided by the Flight for Life team. Visits from eye and heart specialists were common. He even graduated from an isolette to an actual crib. Through it all, he made the greatest gains when Dr. Ben and Taylor were together.

After four-and-a-half months, leaving the NICU was an unimaginable task. We had originally arrived on a Flight for Life, resided for a big block of time at the Ronald McDonald House, and hadn't even tried to take care of ourselves for four months. We were institutionalized. The NICU staff ordered us to make a dry run: pack up bags, spend the night in a regular hospital room, and practice our long-awaited departure.

I had trouble sleeping that night in the hospital. I dropped out of bed and decided to visit Liam. I quietly walked into the NICU and was stopped short by the gentle scene before me. Taylor was in a rocking chair with her eyes closed. She was holding Liam, rocking him slowly. Eyes still closed, she craned her neck and gently kissed the top of his head. Liam sighed. I wasn't troubled or jealous. This was the young woman who had instilled within me the idea that he was strong—strong enough to make it, strong enough to live.

The next morning, we were surprised to meet a television reporter and her cameraman. They wanted an interview with Liam, his doctor, and some of the nurses. Normally, we would have immediately rejected such a request, but today it seemed appropriate. His stay in the NICU was synthesized to a thirty-second piece that focused mostly on the hospital and their investments in technology and not what made it a great place—the learned, caring doctors and nurses. When the reporters left, we passed around pieces of cake to the other parents in the NICU. Everyone was proud of Liam's progress, and we were happy that he was able to leave the hospital. Our fears were calmed by the realization and excitement that we would get to do what most parents do when their child is only a few days old—take him home.

After taking obligatory photographs of Liam with what seemed like everyone at St. Joe's, we were escorted outside. We strapped him in his car seat, and as we were saying our final goodbyes, I realized I had left my camera upstairs. I hurried back inside, stepped off the elevator at the eleventh floor, and briskly walked toward the NICU. I glanced at the open door to the nurse's staffing room and witnessed something that was never meant for my eyes. Holding each other in a supportive embrace were Christine and Taylor, his two primary nurses, tears on both their cheeks. Over the first four months of his life, Liam caused unimaginable stresses and panics, puzzling us with medical anomalies; but most of all, he gave us all someone to love and admire and a very precious reason to celebrate—not just as parents, but as doctors and nurses as well. Taylor was right. He was strong, strong enough to survive, strong enough to live. As Carin and I celebrated bringing our son home, the nurses were left to cope with farewells and with the other fragile lives in their care.

THE GRANDMOTHER'S STORY

I remember my mother's prayers and they have always followed me.
They have clung to me all my life.
—ABRAHAM LINCOLN

Our love for our children is so profound that we do everything we can to protect them. As my children grew, over and over again, I tried to place an imaginary magic circle of safety around them, only to awaken to the reality that any such concept is an illusion. However, prayers to God and prayers to their guardian angels were often part of my consciousness, providing them an ethereal safety net. Years later, I knew that the desire to pray for them and shelter them does not change when they become adults but simply takes on different hues and textures, becoming more complicated and complex according to their life circumstances. Whatever spiritual help I was able to give them so often seemed to not be enough.

At no time in my life was that so clear as on the morning my husband and I stood outside the hospital, watching the Flight for Life medical crew. They were loading the gurney carrying our daughter-in-law, Carin, who was twenty-four weeks into her first pregnancy, into the ambulance. Our son, Barrett, was standing by the ambulance door. He looked shell-shocked as he waited to climb in after her for the short ride to the airport and a date with the plane that would fly them over the mountains to a large Denver hospital.

The next four days were spent monitoring Carin and the baby and reading her vital signs. My own sense of helplessness and emotional dismay grew with each passing day. Finally, late at night, her situation became critical, and the doctors knew it was time to deliver the baby by C-section. I was awakened from a sound sleep very early the next morning with a phone call from my son, saying they had a son and that he was alive but very, very small, weighing just 1 lb. 13 oz. What happened in the 114 days that followed retaught me an age-old lesson: one day at a time, sometimes one hour at a time, is the only way to proceed.

After talking briefly to our other two sons to share the news of the birth, and arranging to take leave from work and to have our dog cared for, my husband and I began the 270 mile drive across the wintry mountain roads to Denver. Dan had packed for a short stay because he doesn't do well in big cities. I packed for a week or so, knowing that I wouldn't be able to leave my son and his new son behind until things were more settled for both of them and for Carin. There was a multitude of questions to be answered and concerns to be voiced that only a whole host of hospital professionals could properly address.

The first sight of the tiny baby, who was no bigger than my son's outspread hand, literally took my breath away. A wave of incomparable raw pain sliced through me. A variety of tubes and wires were attached to his body, giving him life support. I experienced an unparalleled helpless feeling and found myself wondering how much deeper were the new parents' emotions. I thought that a person doesn't need to travel to the moon to experience a whole new world and a never-imagined atmosphere. Constant buzzers and alarms assailed our ears with a subdued but troublesome cacophony. The artificial lighting above the isolette bathed the tiny boy's fragile body in an eerie, harsh glow: a drastic switch from the cozy surroundings of the in-utero warmth he had recently been forced to leave much too early. I was left speechless and struggled to keep my own tears at bay.

Medical personnel had assured the parents that the baby was in no imminent danger, but that there would be a long and perhaps very rocky road to travel during the next hours and days. There would be innumerable doctors and nurses caring for the baby and informing the parents, and advocating for them, as well. I learned within the next weeks that these people were among the most skilled and caring individuals that I had ever known.

Barrett and Carin discussed having their son baptized while I was with them. The result of this conversation was they asked to see the chaplain on call, who arranged for contact with the Catholic chaplain. He came to visit the following day and spent about fifteen minutes with the three of us. The next day, on the fourth day after birth, he met us in the NICU for the baptism. It was an uninspiring thirty-second ceremony. We all knew that it was a conditional baptism and a formal ceremony would have to take place at home for the baptism to become official for the church. Nevertheless, I felt some comfort that William Michael had been proclaimed a child of God by an official member of the clergy, but I also felt much more disquiet because of the minimalist experience with the priest. I was sure he was a very good man, and I understood that he had been pulled out of his teaching retirement to do the baptism. I was quite certain he was a good history teacher because of our conversation during his first visit, but from my perspective, he was not at all equipped to give anything that resembled spiritual care.

I was seeing the whole baptism experience through the eyes of a person who had worked for twenty years for my local Catholic parish. The last six of these years had been as Pastoral Assistant, so I had spent many hours in hospital settings, keeping company with worried family members or with very ill parishioners. Often I was with them when death occurred or was called to the bedside immediately following a death. I worked routinely with people to help them make funeral arrangements for their loved ones, and I visited new parents right after a birth had occurred. Many of these births were joyous happenings, but some were not. Prayer experiences with such people were a routine part of my work, and it bothered me that the priest hadn't even offered a prayer for the parents or the baby during either of his visits, much less ask either of the parents how well they were coping. It was in reflecting upon the whole baptism experience that the seeds for this book were planted.

During the next few days, while I was still in Denver, I tried to sit back and be a quiet, supportive presence as much as possible. I have found through the years that words often get in the way or have an eerie way of being poorly chosen and spoken, or are interpreted wrongly by the recipient. This is especially true in times of stress. It is often a wiser choice to say nothing.

During times away from the hospital, I became reflective and reminiscent. Years ago, I had given birth vaginally three times within a five-year period, and I remembered well the emotional and physical aftermath of those sacred and profound experiences. I had had to deal with particularly difficult emotional trauma after the birth of our third son. So I worried greatly about Carin and marveled at the strength she was showing as she dealt with much more than I had with three births combined. I prayed for her emotional stability, and for my son's, and for so many other things related to this emergency birth. And I was well aware, I had no wisdom based on a birth such as this that I could share with them.

I sat and watched Barrett and Carin grapple with their own roller coaster of emotions. Sometimes I marveled that they were "holding it together" so well, and other times I had to leave them alone for periods of time, concerned that their upsets or tears would be a display they later regretted being witnessed, or that my own tears and heavy heart might add to their burden. I wanted only to bring them whatever positive and hopeful support I had within me.

All too soon my week's time was up, and I left for home a couple of days before Carin was released from the hospital. She would join Barrett, who had been staying with good friends. Just the day before, I had learned that he would be staying on in Denver with her and not returning to a transitional job he was holding before going back to school to get his teaching certification. I worried about the financial burden his unemployment would add to their future. He and I spoke about finances once, but I kept most of my fears to myself, trusting that there was higher guidance going on than I was able to provide.

I returned to Montrose to resume normal life and to help out on the home front by getting their house in order for their several-months absence. My husband and I dismantled their Christmas tree and packed away their holiday decorations for what was to have been their first Christmas in their first house. I was distracted and fought low spirits for days. Our Christmas was very low key and other-focused that year. The melody and words of the nineteenth-century children's lullaby, "Away in the Manger," circled from my mind and through my heart in a continuous stream that season. Some of the words in the third verse became a prayer I uttered over and over again for Liam, who could not pray for himself. "Be near me, Lord Jesus, I ask you to stay... Bless all the dear children in thy tender care." His incredible little life, and the NICU routine that these three loved family members were experiencing, captured most of the positive energy and intention I had within me, though I did return to my part-time work. It provided me a welcome distraction.

Daily phone contacts were a routine I established very quickly. I was horrified to hear of the baby's continued weight loss and worried constantly what permanent effect oxygen deprivation would have on his future brain function. We were hungry for news of progress in the baby's weight gain and wanted badly to hear that both parents were managing well. They spoke of the doctors and nurses more like close friends, but that was understandable, since many of their waking moments were spent in the hospital. I was so glad to hear of this support in spite of the scary information the doctors often imparted. I tried to put my worries in perspective, realizing that doctors must give full disclosure to all possibilities in medical situations. Drawing upon my deep-seated faith in a benevolent and merciful God was very helpful to me, as was my knowing that God was working actively through the minds, hearts, and hands of the medical personnel.

One of the best things we heard about was the Kangaroo Care that both parents and the baby were engaged in. One or the other of the parents would spend an hour or two daily with the tiny child clad in diaper only lying upon their bare chest. This practice is the closest the baby can come to an in-utero experience, and it was something both parents said was the best part of their day.

In reflecting upon this, I realized that very few fathers have the chance to experience such closeness with their child as it grows to normal birth weight. Kangaroo Care was an astoundingly great gift to Barrett. I've watched the tenderness with which he speaks to Liam, and also heard the firmness and conviction in his voice, and seen the pride on his face as he watched his son's small physical accomplishments. I believe it has made him a very different sort of father than he would have been without it, and I feel the results of having been together in Kangaroo Care have formed an inseparable bond between my son and grandson that will grow deeper and stronger during the coming years.

Carin's mother kept us current with e-mailed photos from time to time, and we took photos on our two subsequent visits to Denver. Slowly, I began to put together a photo-journal where the baby's progress was documented. It grew with words and other pictures, with poems, memorabilia, and the formal birth announcement. Writing has always provided me an outlet when deep emotions or worries need to be released. The journal suited that purpose and gave me something to show to people who asked about Liam's progress. Each small step was cause to celebrate, and I wanted to be able to join with others in grateful celebration often. It was this photo-journal that inspired me to consider writing what might become a children's book, with the infant telling his story from conception to leaving the hospital. The result is the story that appears on the flip side of this book.

Each of our two short visits to Denver was a bright spot in the long months, though by the second visit, the strain on Barrett and Carin was apparent. The chance to see Liam's progress firsthand did wonders to instill confidence in his future, and it was simply fantastic when he was big enough for me to hold him during our second visit. There were awkward moments, trying to adjust to the wires and tubes, and words do not do justice to the amount of warmth and tenderness that flowed through me to Liam with him in my arms for the first time. Conversely, in talking with his parents, it was easy to understand how the strain of living out of a suitcase for so long—depending on the hospitality of friends and doing a less-than-wonderful stint at the Ronald McDonald House—was taking its toll. These factors, plus the growing financial worries that were starting to become a reality with each added day of the hospital stay, were causing a pervasive low-current tension between Barrett and Carin. I worried about their relationship and well-being. I had these concerns, in addition to the progress of Liam, to hold in prayer as spring approached.

Helping to prepare for their homecoming was helpful to me as well as to them. They had hoped to refinish their wood floors in the living and dining area before the baby was born, but the early emergency flight to Denver interfered with those plans. They knew Liam would return to Montrose on oxygen and his breathing would be an ongoing concern, so this job needed to be done before Liam was released. Barrett came home for a weekend, and he and his brother, Brian, rented a sander to strip off the old varnish. During the following ten days or so, all of my spare time was spent on my hands and knees, finish-sanding the parts of the floor that would not be covered with an area rug. Carin's mother and I did a few other things, too, to try to prepare for a pleasant homecoming.

It was also important to me to help disseminate information to friends and other community members who were offering such incredible support. The photo-journal helped with this, but I felt a special burden about my daughter-in-law's workplace. She had left her second grade classroom on a Tuesday after school for a routine doctor's appointment, fully expecting to be there on Wednesday. The children arrived the next morning to the news that their teacher was in the hospital. Through the next several days, appropriate information was passed on to the students through the principal and substitute teacher. After the baby's birth, the teacher had the students make artwork greeting cards, which ended up decorating the walls of the NICU. At one point, I made thank-you posters from mother and baby, complete with a Kangaroo Care photograph, to hang in the children's classroom and the teacher's lounge. The response at her workplace was a wonderful microcosm of what happened in the larger community. People everywhere expressed their concern and support with cards, visits, prayers, flowers, and offers of financial help. It seemed to me at one point that there was hardly a soul in town who had not sent their well-wishes to the new parents and tiny baby.

The experiences of their 114 days in Denver reaffirmed to me the goodness inherent within most people. Our son, daughter-in-law, and now 7 lb. 14 oz. baby boy finally waved goodbye to their strong support system at the hospital in Denver and traveled over the mountains to begin family life anew. There would be many adjustments to make. Here they would find strength and support of a different kind from friends, community members, and nearby family members. Words again failed to express my joy and happiness at having them safely home as a threesome.

I have other grandchildren whose lives are equally precious to me as my preemie grandson. My heart has an infinite capacity for love for my children and grandchildren, and there could never be any question about loving one more than the other. But it seemed to me that this homecoming needed a unique kind of celebration to include all the family and some close friends. Once the nicely grown preemie and his parents had a chance to settle in and establish a comfortable routine, I hoped to interest them in having a gathering to give thanks and celebrate their homecoming—a formal ceremony, followed by a party. The ritual was me responding to the call of my soul.

The goal of the ceremony would be to express joy and gratitude for the many hurdles that had been overcome and the resiliency of these first-time parents whose lives had been turned upside down. It was about the fact that the long vigil was finally over and a new phase of life was beginning. It would provide an opportunity to honor the Sacred Source from which all life comes. It would be a chance to unite the spirits of all those who gathered with us, as well as recognize that we all have this same Source around us and within us. It was about including everyone in my overflowing relief, praise, and thanksgiving. There was, indeed, much to celebrate.

THE GRANDFATHER'S STORY

What a bargain grandchildren are! I give them my loose change, and they give
me a million dollars' worth of pleasure.
—GENE PERRET

I once believed that many grandfathers and prospective grandfathers of
my generation suffer from the same dilemma: we love our children and
find the prospect of grandfatherhood a pleasant one, but we also suffer
from a certain detachment, uncertain how to react to pregnant women
or newborn babies. It's easy enough to ask how a mom is doing and to
hold a baby and make silly faces and noises, but there is always a sense of
awkwardness. This has certainly been the case with me.

And so I was quite surprised at my emotional and intellectual reac-
tion when it was discovered there were serious complications related to
the birth of the baby expected by our youngest son, Barrett, and his wife,
Carin. Our prospective mom had preeclampsia, a condition with which
I was totally unfamiliar. When I learned more about it from our ever-
faithful family *Merck Manual*, my concern escalated.

Mom entered our small-town hospital during her fifth month, and
when we went to visit, she looked perfectly fine, if not a little frightened.
In a few days, the doctor said otherwise and made the decision to fly
mother and unborn baby to Denver, where she might get the kind of care
that would allow her to carry the baby until he was more ready to enter
the world.

We watched as the Flight for Life crew loaded her on a gurney and
pushed it rumbling down the hall. They were kind and professional, people you instantly know can be trusted to do everything right in taking care
of your family. In spite of that, a terrible emptiness comes at those times,
and countless questions raced through my mind. Would Carin and baby

be able to tolerate the flight? Would they arrive safely? How would Barrett and she react if in fact they lost this baby? How would my spouse react? How would I? Would our son remain in Denver until the baby came? And would the insurance cover all the expenses?

Mother, father, and baby made the trip just fine, and young Liam was born a few days later, weighing in at a staggeringly small 1 lb. 13 oz. Once again, my mind raced with confused and often nonsensical emotions. I also spent a good deal of time trying to figure out just how big a less-than-two-pound baby might be. Would he really fit in the palm of my hand, as I had heard? We drove over the mountains to see this miracle child and offer what support we could to Barrett and Carin.

Mom was in her hospital bed when we arrived in Denver, and my awkwardness reasserted itself. How are you feeling? How is the baby doing? What am I supposed to feel or say? Why am I so frightened? We also learned that young Liam was facing many problems other than low birth weight.

We visited with Carin for a while, and then Barrett took us to the NICU. It took only seconds to realize that this huge room was filled with babies in plastic boxes—then seconds more to realize that each plastic box had by its side moms and dads, or just dads, or solo moms. Nurses and doctors were everywhere, scurrying from box to box. I did as we were told and just followed our son to Liam's box, trying not to stare at the other boxes or all the activity taking place. The moment of truth had come.

And yes, Liam would fit in the palm of my hand, or would have had he not been attached to so many wires and tubes. They were in his nose and in his mouth, coming from his hands and his feet, all leading to myriad machines keeping his scrawny redness alive. The lights on the machines flashed ominously, as did those up and down the aisles with their many plastic boxes. Every few minutes, alarms would sound near one of the boxes, and nurses, sometimes doctors, would fly into motion. I found myself more fearful than at any other time in my life. Barrett explained that the alarms warned that babies had stopped breathing or that their oxygen levels had dropped to a dangerous low. I stared at this totally helpless and dependent baby who could neither breathe on his own nor suck in nourishment, this baby whose feet seemed to be oversized for his miniscule body, and I thought of Oliver Twist: "Please, sir, could I have more?"

Liam in no way resembled the happy, chubby babies on a baby food jar. He was so terribly tiny and frail. And in that moment, I knew there was no way this baby could live. Barrett told us that there were, indeed, problems. Liam might need surgery to repair a hole in his heart. His brain was bleeding. His lungs were underdeveloped for his size, and his future eyesight was threatened. With all this, Liam didn't cry. Babies *should* cry. And for the first time since my own children were born, one of whom was hospitalized in another town, I asked God for a huge favor.

Two young women, nurses, were caring for Liam. *Two*, not one. And I was astounded at the love and skill they lavished upon that baby. They are living, walking saints, and I hope they are still there caring for other little Liams. It is a miracle that they are able to do their jobs day after day, loving the babies and being so kind to frantic moms and dads. It's an even bigger miracle that they are willing to let the babies, in whom they have so much of themselves invested, go home with their parents. And that is the biggest miracle. These babies do grow, flourish, and go home. Certainly, many have some problems to overcome, just as Liam and his mom and dad did. But they do go home together.

The months after Liam came home are something of a blur. When Carin went back to work, his grandmother and I kept Liam one day a week. And during that first year, my awkwardness returned. It was nice to hold him and make silly faces in hope that he would smile. Oddly enough, I felt closer to him in many ways than I did my own children. His heart healed itself, and his brain stopped bleeding. He put on weight and moved and squirmed and wiggled and pooped. His miniature lungs remained a problem for quite some time, but his eyesight continued to improve. He began a course of physical therapy to develop his motor skills. This therapy continued at home, where we gently brushed his arms, legs, and back with a very soft brush of nylon bristles. He was so tender and tiny that I worried the brush would hurt him, although it obviously did not. He finally did cry when something really hurt but the rest of the time he was full of smiles.

Liam is six years old now—healthy, happy, active, smart, and with nearly normal lungs. He has an almost adult-level sense of humor, is learning to enjoy jokes, and overall has an incredibly sunny, friendly disposition. He skis with his mom and dad at Telluride and has become one of those amazing youngsters who zooms down hills, totally embarrassing or annoying less-skilled adults. Liam and his dad went pheasant hunting with me last winter when the temperature was in the low twenties and snow covered the ground. Liam carried a big, frozen stick just in case a pheasant flew up near him. He only fell one time and immediately bounced up and continued on. He tagged along for three hours, marching through grass and weeds higher than his head and jabbering constantly: "Hey, Papa, you know what?" Well, Liam, you know what? Your Neeo and I love you more than anything. People all over town love you, Liam, and you will grow to do great things.

William

*Now there's William. He comes pecking, like a bird, at my
heart. His eyebrows are like the feathers of a wren. His ears
are little seashells.*

I would keep him always in my mind's eye.

*Soon enough he will be tall, walking and conversing; he'll have
ideas, and a capricious will; the passions will unfold in him,
like greased wheels, and he will leap forward upon them.*

*Who knows, maybe he'll be an athlete, quick and luminous;
or a musician, bent like a long-legged pin over the piano's
open wing; or maybe he will stand day after day over a drafts-
man's desk, making something exquisite and useful—a tower
or a bridge.*

*Whatever he does, he'll want the world to do it in. Maybe,
who knows, he'll want this very room which, only for con-
venience, I realize, I've been calling mine.*

*I feel myself begin to wilt, like an old flower,
weak in the stem.*

*But he is irresistible! Whatever he wants of mine—my room,
my ideas, my glass of milk, my socks and shirt, my place in
line, my portion, my world—he may have it.*

—Mary Oliver from *White Pine, Poems and Prose Poems*

Table setting for the Welcome Home ceremony.

APPENDIX A

Welcome Home Ceremony

A Welcome Home ceremony provides a special occasion to invite all family members, as well as a few close friends who gave strong support during the time in the hospital, to join together to celebrate. A ceremony is a way to formally welcome the child into the family, and to provide the parents with any opportunity to once again express their joy in their child's progress and their gratitude to those who bolstered them during those difficult weeks or months.

Create the environment for the ceremony to reflect the parents' experiences since the birth of the child. In this example, the central table is adorned with several meaningful elements. A stained-glass purple heart and purple heart-shaped confetti symbolize an anonymous gift the parents received. Pictures represent the medical staff that supported them so well and the relatives for whom the child was named. A scattering of dollar bills will be distributed to the participants as a way for the parents to anonymously send back into the larger community their gratitude and thanksgiving while uplifting the lives of others. Candles are placed on and around the table and are lit to begin the celebration. Chairs for participants are arranged in a circle around the table, which is draped in a green cloth.

A close friend or family member would be the ideal person to lead the ceremony—someone who is comfortable speaking in front of people and who has a basic understanding of ritual. The person who developed the ritual is often the leader. Alternatively, a pastor, rabbi, or head of a congregation would likely be willing to lead the ceremony, but, as a courtesy, include that person in the planning. Allow plenty of time for the person to schedule his or her involvement.

Identify two people who are comfortable and read well in a group setting. Give them a script so they can practice it, ideally a day before the gathering. Give them programs so they will know when their reading will take place.

This example reflects a Catholic tradition. For example, it includes references to guardian angels and the communion of saints, both important to the Catholic faith, and explains their relevance to our family's experience.

Welcome Home

A Ritual for a Premature Baby, Family, and Friends

Words of Welcome
The leader welcomes those who have come and briefly explains why a formal ceremony is being held. He or she tells the participants what the ritual includes: scripture, a story, music, two readings, storytelling by those present, and brief prayers.

Opening Prayer: God of Life and Love, we gather today to welcome this precious child, _____, into the _____ and _____ families. It is with great joy and happiness that we look down upon a healthy boy/girl after all the worries, fears, and challenges of these last few months. Send your Spirit of joy and hope among us as we celebrate this homecoming. Amen.

A Reading: Psalms 139: 1-6, 13-15

Yahweh, you search me and know me,
You know if I am standing or sitting.
You perceive my thoughts from far away.
Whether I walk or lie down, you are watching;
You are familiar with all my ways.

Before a word is even on my tongue, Yahweh,
You know it completely.
Close behind and close in front, you hem me in,
Shielding me with your hand.
Such knowledge is beyond my understanding,
Too high beyond my reach.

You created my inmost being
And knit me together in my mother's womb.
For all these mysteries—
For the wonder of myself,
For the wonder of your works—
I thank you.

You know me through and through
From having watched my bones take shape,
When I was being formed in secret,
Woven together in the womb.

from *Psalms Anew* by Nancy Schreck, OSF, and Maureen Leach, OSF

Music: "Before I Was Born" by David Haas (from the CD *Before I Was Born*, Chicago, GIA Publications, 1999)

Reading and Storytelling: *Angel in the Waters* by Regina Doman

This is a children's book about a baby in the womb, his exploration of the waters, and his conversation with an angel who is with him there.
Read and display pp. 1-13 to "When things did not move, I did."

This is where the story diverges from this storybook. Tell briefly of the events that led to the premature birth. Offer a thought or two about what parents went through when they learned the baby would be coming so early. Mention that angels and saints have been a supportive reality during the past weeks. Invite the parents to share a few words.

A Reading: *Preemie Purple Heart* by Renea Ericson (www.preemiepurple-heart.com)

A glass purple heart pendant with a teardrop, along with this reading, was left anonymously in my grandchild's crib in the NICU two days after his birth. My daughter-in-law wore the heart for many months following. It reappeared following another very trying pregnancy, and is still worn at special times of remembrance. .

One day a child was born, too early, too small but loved as much as any child could be. As the parents of this child entered this journey they found themselves feeling alone. They had the joys of being new parents but the fear of losing their child, this thrill of giving birth, the grief of a lost dream. This was supposed to be a joyous time, not a time filled with grief, anger and pain. Little did they know they were not alone.

The Preemie Purple Heart is born of an idea, borrowed from the U.S. Army, a medal given for being wounded in battle. What bigger battle is there than the battle for life?... [T]he wounds of premature birth live on with the infant and family... The color was once reserved for royalty, making it special and its gender neutral. The heart is not a solid color and the stripes in each heart are a little different, just as every child and every journey is a little different, but the basic design is the same, just as the basic experience is the same. The heart is made of glass and is strong, but not so strong it could withstand a crushing blow. The premature child is strong but not invincible. It is a heart because the heart is our center, its every beat renews life and hope, it symbolizes love. At the bottom of the purple heart is a teardrop; it symbolizes the tears shed during the journey of a premature family; good and bad, joy and sorrow.

The Preemie Purple Heart is an outward sign of unity among a special group of people. This is a group that knows no country, language, economic, ethnic, or religious bounds; a group with one common goal: hope for the future of premature children. This group includes not only parents and child, but siblings, grandparents, aunts, uncles, cousins, nurses, doctors, clergy, and friends. This group shares a bond beyond words, a bond only the heart knows. The heart can be with you when you feel alone, reminding you there are hundreds of others who keep you in their hearts. It can give you a chance to share your story.

Expression of Gratitude: Distribution of Dollar Bills

Before the service, determine the number of dollar bills that each person can take. Children are delighted to have the opportunity to spend their dollar bills to help out another person. It is important that this part of the ritual be conducted in a solemn, joyful, and unhurried way, especially if there are many children present. After a pause of a few moments following the reading, the leader says:

These dollar bills are a symbol of gratitude and thanksgiving. I invite each of you to take __ dollar bills; please do so slowly and quietly, two or three people coming forward at a time. After you leave today, use them as donations to a good cause or to buy a surprise gift for someone else. In this way, you can help us extend the good that we have experienced back into the community that supported us so well. *(Play music while participants gather their bills.)*

Music: *Play "Suffer the Little Children" from* Healing Angel *by Roma Downey (from the CD Healing Angel, Dublin, Ireland, Westland Studios, 1999), or some other appropriate piece.*

Requests of God
The leader begins by stating a certain quality he or she wishes would become part of the child's being as it grows, such as generosity, laughter, or love of animals. Invite others to share what they would ask God for on behalf of _____.

Closing Blessing
Extend a hand in blessing over the child.

As you grow, may you be blessed with many of these qualities. Throughout the years to come, may your path be one of goodness, and may you continue to be the source of joy, light, and inspiration to all whom you meet. May God's angels continue to travel with you. Welcome to our family, sweet _____. Amen.

Extinguish candles and thank participants for coming. To help people move from a solemn atmosphere to a more festive one, play "We Are Family" by Sister Sledge, or another favorite family oriented piece of music.

Serve refreshments.

There are two other wonderful children's storybooks that would work well in a ritual or to use as a hopeful, peaceful interlude in the NICU. Both have an audio CD with beautiful music included in the book. They are:

John Denver's For Baby (For Bobbie), adapted and illustrated by Janeen Mason.

Over the Rainbow, performed by Judy Collins with paintings by Eric Puybaret.

APPENDIX B

Prayers & Poems

PRAYERS

Parents' Prayer

Creator God, it is unknown to us why things have come together in such a way that _____ was born so small and fragile. We seek answers for many questions and face untold fears. We turn to you with our anxieties, as well as our hopes and dreams for our future as a family, and place all of these in your tender care. Bless us and our very small daughter/son, _____, as well as her/his brothers/sisters (if any). Amen.

Journaling suggestion: Write your own prayers in the blank lines which follow each of these four prayers.

Prayer for Parents

God of compassion, I/we uplift to you _____and_____ as they deal with their child's sudden and unexpected birth. Give them the strength, courage, and insight they need to handle the next few days/ weeks. Ease their fears and anxieties and strengthen their spirits and bodies. May other family members (friends) who offer them support be sensitive to their needs and faithful in their care. I/we ask this with faith in your guiding providence. Amen.

Prayer for Caregivers

Healer God, the tiny life of _____ is in the skilled hands of many different doctors and nurses now. Help them work together to make the very best decisions to promote the comfort and steady growth for little _____. Inspire and direct them. Guide their minds, hearts, and hands and make them your instruments of healing and health today and in the days to come. Amen.

_____

_____

_____

_____

_____

_____

_____

_____

_____

_____

_____

_____

_____

_____

Grandparent's Prayer

Merciful God, it is so difficult and painful to watch my child, who is unexpectedly the father/mother of a newly born premature child, deal with this trauma. All of his/her dreams of giving birth to a healthy, robust infant are now replaced with grief and anxieties. I beg for your wisdom in knowing how to give support to him/her and his/her spouse. Inspire my words when I feel called to speak, and help me know when it is best to remain a silent presence. Amen.

_____

_____

_____

_____

_____

_____

_____

_____

_____

_____

_____

_____

_____

_____

_____

POEMS

For Baby (For Bobbie)

I'll walk in the rain by your side,
I'll cling to the warmth of your hand,
I'll do anything to keep you satisfied
I love you more than anybody can.

And the wind will whisper your name to me
little birds will sing along in time,
leaves will bow down when you walk by
and morning bells will chime.

I'll be there when you're feelin' down
to kiss away the tears if you cry,
I'll share with you all the happiness I've found
a reflection of the love in your eyes.

And I'll sing you the songs of the rainbow,
the whisper of the joy that is mine
leaves will bow down when you walk by
and morning bells will chime.

I'll walk in the rain by your side,
I'll cling to the warmth of your tiny hand,
I'll do anything to help you understand
I love you more than anybody can.

And the wind will whisper your name to me
little birds will sing along in time,
leaves will bow down when you walk by
and morning bells will chime.

—John Denver from the album *Rocky Mountain High*

Newborn Fingers

How beautiful new fingers are,
And how complete,
And how far more accomplished
Than baby feet.
Opening and closing
To what dim commands,
Marvelous miniature
The fingers of new hands.
Longing to touch and hold
Already a vital thing,
Else how explain the strength
Of that first grip and cling?
The giver and the grasper
Held within
Ten fragile filaments
Of skin.

—Mary O'Neill from *Fingers Are Always Bringing Me News*

Patience

To wait within is hardest:
To be, while still becoming;
Doomed to all that slowness,
Never once to die.

To wait until tomorrow
Costs but a little sleep.
The wildernesses inward
Takes years to cross.

Nor is the going wasted
If every stretch was loved;
The last hill then is home ground,
For all its light be strange.

—Mark Van Doren from *Collected and New Poems 1924-1963*

Hope

It hovers in dark corners
before the lights are turned on,
  it shakes sleep from its eyes
  and drops from mushroom gills,
    it explodes in the starry heads
    of dandelions turned sages,
        it sticks to the wings of green angels
        that sail from the tops of maples.

It sprouts in each occluded eye
of the many-eyed potato,
  it lives in each earthworm segment
  surviving cruelty,
    it is the motion that runs
    from the eyes to the tail of a dog,
        it is the mouth that inflates the lungs
        of the child that has just been born.

It is the singular gift
we cannot destroy in ourselves,
the argument that refutes death,
the genius that invents the future,
all we know of God.

It is the serum which makes us swear
not to betray one another;
it is in this poem, trying to speak.

—Lisel Mueller from *Alive Together, New and Selected Poems*

Jeffrey's Poem

When I first saw you, kid, you were tiny and thin
And slimy and red and your head was mushed in.
I said to your mother, 'He looks kind of sloppy,
And two pounds four ounces ain't big for a crappie.'

But something about you, the look in your eyes,
Said you fully intended to grow to full size.
They slapped your backside and let you cry,
And I said, 'We will keep him, at least we shall try.'

Some babies are born in nine months, by the clock.
Some babies are born, and they sit up and talk.
Some babies are born and no doctor is there.
But some babies come in on a wing and a prayer.

Poor little fetus as big as your hand.
Poor little fish thrown up on dry land.
Who came in late April though he had 'til July,
Too small to live and too precious to die.

They slipped you downstairs to the big Neonatal
Intensive Care Unit's computerized cradle
And attached you to wires and stuck you with tubes
Monitored closely by digital cubes.

And thanks to the latest neonatal therapeusis
And regular basting with greases from gooses
And hot chicken soup intravenously fed
You did not fade away, you grew up instead.

We'll always remember the months that you spent
With tubes in your head in the oxygen tent
And a mask on your face, the wires attached,
Sweet little baby that was only half hatched.
I'm sure you'll grow up and mature and extend
To six feet six inches and become a tight end,

But I'll always remember each doctor and nurse in
The NICU who helped make you a person,

The kid who crash landed, who was carried away,
Who survived it, this bundle we bring home today.

—Garrison Keillor

The Negro Speaks of Rivers

I've known rivers:
I've known rivers ancient as the world and
    older than the flow of human blood in human veins.

My soul has grown deep like the rivers.

I bathed in the Euphrates when dawns were young.
I built my hut near the Congo and it lulled me to sleep.
I looked upon the Nile and raised pyramids above it.
I heard the singing of the Mississippi when Abe Lincoln
    went down to New Orleans, and I've seen its muddy
    bosom turn all golden in the sunset.

I've known rivers:
Ancient, dusky rivers.

My soul has grown deep like the rivers.

—Langston Hughes from *The Collected Poems of Langston Hughes*

The following seven poems are by Rosemerry Wahtola Trommer
—www.wordwoman.com, www.ahundredfallingveils.wordpress.com

...the Mother Struggles with Regret (excerpt)

It is easy to look back and think
"I could have done better..."

...I try to tell myself you are like a tree
planted in a shadow. You will bend
toward the sun and find a way to thrive.
Nothing can stop you. We are wired
to struggle, to grapple, to twist,
to stretch, to mature, to survive. It is not
the shadows that shape us
but the reaching for the light.

And Then We Smell the Cool Damp of the Creek

We do not always hear the footsteps when sorrow
limps up to our door. Nor does the doorbell ring.
Our signs may say, "Do not disturb, please."

but sorrow is illiterate, untaught in etiquette.
He does not take his black boots off, just walks right in.

Recovery

Even today when tears slip between tears,
when the river ice welds its long chill to the banks
and will not melt till one hundred more mornings have come,
Even now the only thing that makes sense
is to fall more deeply in love.

Mystery at the Door

It's not even distance that matters:
how many miles, how many years,
how many inches on the map. I believe
in the leap, the untying of strings,
the improbable learning to fly.
I believe in the wings that beat in the chest,
the sky concert where song unfolds in the breath.
I believe in praising the ache as it blossoms
in heartbreak's bountiful soils. In scouring.
How a whispered *yes* unleashes ninety-nine butterflies.
A kiss becomes a wave. A blue flame ignites the universe.
Blink. Unblink. Reach. Receive. I believe
in unbuilding walls that we've made.
I believe in opening. Unproving. Praise.

Breathing

I tell myself it is easy to love you, like breathing
I say. Perhaps, but today, it's more like birth,
a red agony laced with ecstatic tang,
more like ocean bathing
with its salty sting. More like the bright ring
of a bell than soft rumor of exhale, more like baring
my skin to the winter full moon and letting the night
touch me everywhere. Goosebumps and hinter
flesh, gasp! A rare thing
to be so aware of each hinge
of inhale, each grin,
each laugh, each moan, wail, sigh. Come near,
my love, and you will hear
how the tide of my heart
is less predictable than breath.
More like a barge
adrift in the waves, seeking a refuge, a berthing.

During the Breathing Meditation

So soon into the
holding, the body
takes over. It does
not care about

my resolve. It
does not care
that I have
have not waited
the seven full counts
before the exhale.
The body does what

a body does,
which is bring
the world in
and release it again.
Effortlessly.
And I come
to see that I
am not the one

doing the breathing.
I am being breathed.
Filled and emptied.
An altar for air.

It is this way
with loving you.

Microcosm

In our palms
our heartbeats
hum in accord
with the wild,
expanding universe,
as if with clap
and clasp and reach
we say, Yes, Universe!
I am your daughter,
I am your son,
I am the acrobat
swimming & pulsing
in your abundant womb,
I am the spinning child—
more whir than bone,
more blur than skin,
more dance than limb—
Universe, as I twirl
and travel inside
your miraculous body,
I add my heartbeat
to yours, pulsing,
ready again
and again
to be born.

Journaling suggestion:

Substitute your child's name for the poem *William* by Mary Oliver, which appears at the end of The Grandfather's Story on p. 83 of this book. Change the gender if need be. Or write your own prose poem using this one as inspiration, then read it to your child.

_____

_____

_____

_____

_____

_____

_____

_____

_____

_____

_____

_____

_____

_____

_____

_____

_____

_____

_____

Bibliography

Books

Arrien, Angeles. *The Four-Fold Way: Walking the Paths of the Warrior, Teacher, Healer and Visionary*. New York: HarperCollins Publishers, 1993.

——. *Holy Bible, The New Revised Standard Version*. Iowa Falls, IA: World Bible Publishers, Inc., 1989.

Biziou, Barbara. *The Joy of Ritual: Spiritual Recipes to Celebrate Milestones, Ease Transitions, and Make Every Day Sacred*. New York: Golden Books, 1999.

Boyer, Mark G. *Seeking Grace in Every Step, The Spirituality of John Denver*. Springfield, MO: Leavenhouse Publications, 1996.

Brazelton, T. Barry, M.D. *Touchpoints: Your Child's Emotional and Behavioral Development*. Reading, MA: Addison-Wesley Publishing Co., 1992.

Carlson, Richard, and Benjamin Shield, eds. *Handbook for the Soul*. Boston: Little, Brown and Company, 1995.

Cole, Joanna. *When You Were Inside Mommy*. San Francisco: HarperCollins Publishers, 2001.

Collins, Judy, performer, and Eric Puybaret, illustrator. *Over the Rainbow*. Morganville, NJ: Imagine Publishing, 2010.

Doman, Regina. *Angel in the Waters*. Manchester, NH: Sophia Institute Press, 2004.

Dossey, Larry, M.D. *Prayer Is Good Medicine: How to Reap the Healing Benefits of Prayer*. San Francisco: HarperCollins, 1996.

Dossey, Larry, M.D., *Recovering the Soul: A Scientific and Spiritual Search*. New York: Bantam Books, 1989.

Dossey, Larry, M.D., *The Extra-Ordinary Healing Power of Ordinary Things: Fourteen Steps to Health and Happiness.* New York: Harmony Books, 1996.

Frey, William H. *Crying: The Mystery of Tears.* Minneapolis, MN: Winston Press, 1985.

Fry, William F. *Sweet Madness: A Study of Humor.* Palo Alto, CA: Pacific Books, 1968.

Gayner, Mitchell L. *Sounds of Healing.* New York: Broadway Books, 1999.

Godwin, Gail. *Heart, A Personal Journey Through Its Myths and Meanings.* New York: William Morrow, 2001.

Goleman, Daniel, Ph.D., and Joel Gurin, eds. *Mind Body Medicine, How to Use Your Mind for Better Health.* Yonkers, NY: Consumer Reports Books, 1993.

Horn, Gabriel. *The Book of Ceremonies: A Native Way of Honoring and Living the Sacred.* Novanto, CA: New World Library, 2000.

Hughes, Langston. *The Collected Poems of Langston Hughes.* Edited by Arnold Rampersad and David Roessel. New York: Vintage Books, 1995.

Isaacs, Gregory, and Sylvester Weise. *Night Nurse.* London, England: Charisma Music Publishing Co., LTD., 1982.

Keillor, Garrison. *Jeffrey's Poem.* Minneapolis, MN: Hangs in the NICU at Abbott Northwestern Hospital.

Kurtz, Ernest, and Katherine Ketcham. *The Spirituality of Imperfection, Modern Wisdom from Classic Stories.* New York: Bantam Books, 1992.

Kushner, Harold S. *When Bad Things Happen to Good People.* New York: Schocken Books, 1981.

Leach, Maureen, OSF, and Nancy Schreck, OSF. *Psalms Anew, In Inclusive Language.* Winona, MN: Saint Mary's Press, 1986.

Lopez, Barry. *Crow and Weasel.* New York: Farrar, Straus and Giroux, A Sunburst Book, 1998.

Madden, Susan L. *The Preemie Parents' Companion: The Essential Guide to Caring for Your Premature Baby in the Hospital, and Through the First Years.* Boston: The Harvard Common Press, 2000.

Mason, Janeen. *John Denver's For Baby (For Bobbie)*, adapted and illustrated. Nevada City, CA: Dawn Publications, 2009.

Moyers, Bill D., Betty S. Flowers, and David Grubin. *Healing and the Mind.* New York: Doubleday, 1993.

Mueller, Lisel. *Alive Together, New & Selected Poems.* Baton Rouge: Louisiana State University Press, 1996.

Murkoff, Heidi, Arlene Eisenberg, and Sandee Hathaway. *What to Expect When You Are Expecting.* New York: Workman Publishing, 2002.

Newberg, Andrew, M.D., Eugene D'Aquili, M.D., and Vince Rause. *Why God Won't Go Away: Brain Science and the Biology of Belief.* New York: Ballantine Publishing Group, 2001.

O'Neill, Mary. *Fingers Are Always Bringing Me News.* Garden City, NY: Doubleday, 1969.

Oliver, Mary. *White Pine, Poems and Prose Poems.* San Diego: Harcourt, Inc., 1994.

Pasquariello, Patrick S., Jr., M.D., ed. *The Children's Hospital of Philadelphia Book of Pregnancy and Child Care.* New York: John Wiley & Sons, Inc., 1999.

Perret, Gene. *Grandchildren Are So Much Fun We Should Have Had Them First.* Phoenix, AZ: WitWorks, 2001.

Rilke, Rainer Maria. *The Selected Poetry of Rainer Maria Rilke*, edited and translated by Stephen Mitchell. New York: Vintage Books, 1989.

Sandeman, Anna. *Babies.* Brookfield, CT: Copper Beech Books, 1996.

Sears, William, M.D., Robert Sears, M.D., James Sears, M.D., and Martha Sears. *The Premature Baby Book: Everything You Need to Know About Your Premature Baby from Birth to Age One.* New York: Little, Brown and Company, 2004.

Speerstra, Karen, ed. *Divine Sparks, Collected Wisdom of the Heart.* Sandpoint, ID: Morning Light Press, 2005.

Van Doren, Mark. *Collected and New Poems, 1924-1963.* New York: Hill and Wang, 1963.

Wall, Kathleen, and Gary Ferguson. *Lights of Passage: Rituals and Rites of Passage for the Problems and Pleasures of Modern Life.* San Francisco: HarperCollins Publishers, 1994.

Wallace, Carol McD. *20,001 Names for Baby.* New York: Avon Books, 1992.

Williamson, Marianne. *Everyday Grace: Having Hope, Finding Forgiveness, and Making Miracles.* New York: Riverhead Books, 2002.

York, Sarah. *Remembering Well: Rituals for Celebrating Life and Mourning Death.* San Francisco: Jossey-Bass, 2000.

Articles

——. "Reading Your Baby's Mind," *Newsweek*, April 15, 2005, pp. 32-39.

——. "Walking in the Womb," BBC News, June 28, 2004, as reported in *National Catholic Register*, July 18-24, 2004.

Music Albums

Daquioag, William, producer. "Waimea Lullaby" by Patrick Downs, "Flying With Angels" by Lehua Kalima, and several instrumentals. *Hawaiian Lullabies.* Waipahu, Hawaii: World Music, 1999.

Denver, John. "For Baby (for Bobbie)." *Rocky Mountain High.* RCA, 1972.

Downey, Roma, and Phil Coulter. "Suffer the Little Children." *Healing Angel.* Dublin, Ireland: Westland Studios, 1999.

Hass, David. "Before I Was Born." *Before I Was Born.* Chicago: GIA Publications, 1999.

Jacobs, Tom. *Songs in the Key of Hope.* Tom Jacobs Productions, 2003.

Montgomery, Doug. "What a Wonderful World." *Me & My Baby Grand.* Santa Fe, NM: DM013, 1999.

Sherman, Kathy, CSJ. "The Heart Knows," "I'll Just Sit Here With You," "Be At Peace," and "Sometimes." *The Heart Knows.* LaGrange, IL: Ministry of the Arts, 2000.

MP-3 Music Downloads

"The Prayer" by Josh Groban and Charlotte Church

"Perhaps Love" and "For Baby (for Bobbie)" by John Denver

"Somewhere Over the Rainbow" by various artists

Websites

Ericson, Renea. www.preemiepurpleheart.com

Jacobs, Tom. www.tomjacobs.com

Sherman, Kathy. www.ministryofthearts.com

Trommer, Rosemerry Wahtola. www.wordwoman.com, www.ahundredfallingveils.wordpress.com

Resources for Ritual*

Cameron, Julia. *Heart Steps, Prayers & Declarations for a Creative Life*. East Rutherford, NJ: Penguin Putnam, Inc., 1997.

Cleary, William. *Prayers to She Who Is*. New York: Crossroad Publishing Co., 1997.

Craughwell, Thomas K., ed. "Every Eye Beholds You." *A World Treasury of Prayers*. New York: Harcourt Brace & Company, 1998.

Geitz, Elizabeth, et al, eds. *Women's Uncommon Prayers, Our Lives Revealed, Nurtured, Celebrated*. Harrisburg, PA: Morehouse Publishing, 2000.

Hays, Edward. *Prayers for a Planetary Pilgrim, A Personal Manual for Prayer and Ritual*. Easton, KS: Forest of Peace Books, Inc., 1988.

Horn, Gabriel. *The Book of Ceremonies, A Native Way of Honoring and Living the Sacred*. Novato, CA: New World Library, 2000.

Oman, Maggie, et al, eds. *Prayers for Healing, 365 Blessings, Poems, & Meditations for Around the World*. Berkeley, CA: Conari Press, 1997.

Roberts, Elizabeth, and Elias Amidon. *Life Prayers from Around the World: 365 Prayers, Blessings, & Affirmations to Celebrate the Human Journey*. New York: HarperCollins Publishers, 1996.

Rupp, Joyce. *Prayers to Sophia, A Companion to Star in My Heart*. Philadelphia, PA: Innisfree Press, Inc., 2000.

Seaburg, Carl. *Great Occasions: Readings for the Celebration of Birth, Coming of Age, Marriage & Death*. Boston, MA: Skinner House Books, 1998.

Simons, Thomas G. *Blessings for God's People*. Norte Dame, IN: Ave Maria Press, 1983.

Tickle, Phyllis, compiler. *The Divine Hours, A Manual for Prayer.* 3 vols. New York: Doubleday, 2000.

* Libraries, the hospital chaplain, and the Internet are helpful for families in finding additional resources. Any bible or holy book and selected books of poetry are good sources.

Glossary of
Medical Terms

Apnea—The absence of breathing; temporary stopping of respiration.

C-PAP—Abbreviation for Continuous Positive Airway Pressure. A respiratory therapy that forces air into the nasal passages, keeping airways open and delivering air to the lungs.

D-sat—An abbreviation for the desaturation of oxygen that is carried by hemoglobin in the bloodstream; values below 90%.

Eclampsia—An acute and life-threatening complication of pregnancy causing high blood pressure and toxemia, which lead to convulsions (seizures).

Intubation—Insertion of a tube into a hollow organ or passageway, often into the airway or into the stomach through the throat or nasal cavity.

Isolette—A clear plastic, enclosed bassinet used to keep prematurely born infants warm. Also called an incubator.

Kangaroo Care—Skin-to-skin contact between the baby's front and the mother or father's chest. The more skin the better; for comfort, a small diaper and cap for the infant is often used.

Neonatal Intensive Care Unit (NICU)—An intensive care unit that specializes in the care of critically ill newborn babies.

Ob-gyn—An abbreviation for medical doctors who specialize in obstetrics and gynecology.

Preeclampsia—A condition with symptoms of increasingly high blood pressure that leads to critical or life-threatening seizures.

Ventilator—A mechanical device used to administer oxygen artificially to patients unable to breathe on their own.

BIOGRAPHICAL INFORMATION

The Author:

Sharon Beshoar has a Masters Degree in Community Leadership from Regis University. She was Associate Pastor at Saint Mary's Church in Montrose, CO from 1990–1996 where hospital chaplaincy was a routine duty. Following that, she volunteered as an intern Spiritual Caregiver with the Hospice of the Uncompahgre Valley for two years. Currently she is semi-retired and employed part time by the Montrose Regional Library District, where she marvels at the incredible world of information and imagination available to young people today.

Liam and his grandmother, Sharon, aka "Neo"

The End

All endings are beginnings of new and different things.
Flip this book over to enter the imaginary world of William
at the beginning of his life.

Liam with his parents in 2007

Photos © Brenda Metheny, www.boocreations.com

Visit my website and blog at www.prematurebirthheartwork.com to:

— share your own experiences and ways of coping with a premature birth

— read comments from professionals and their reactions to the book

— hear a portion of Tom Jacobs' music from "Songs in the Key of Hope"

TO PLACE ORDERS:

Order directly from the author with discounts for
professionals for multiple copies by e-mailing
sharonbeshoar@gmail.com or by mail to the following address:

Heart Works
61401 Lobo Dr.
Montrose, CO 81403

To place a credit card order, go to Amazon.com.

WILLIAM and the NICU

Text by Sharon Beshoar

Illustrations by Kevin F. Novack

LIFETIME CHRONICLE PRESS/dba
LONDON PUBLISHING~
Montrose, CO

www.prematurebirthheartwork.com

To order copies of the book, see page 121

First edition
Printed in the United States of America

Library of Congress Control Number: 2011935306
ISBN: 978-0-9822935-9-1

Cover and book design by Laurie Goralka Design
Illustrations by Kevin F. Novack
Visit Kevin on his Facebook page at Kevin F. Novack Fine Art

London Publishing
10614 Bostwick Park Rd.
Montrose, CO 81401
970-240-1153
chronicle@montrose.net
www.londonpublishing.net

The Baby's Story

A baby is God's opinion that the world
should go on.

—CARL SANDBURG

3

My life begins in
a shadowy place
when the work of
God, along with
my parents' love,
join together
on a starlit
summer's night.
I find myself in
the comfort of
silky fluid and
quiet dark, much
like life begins
for all boys and
girls around the
world.

5-10 Weeks Old

Inside my mom's
tummy, I am warm
and cozy. I swim
and am nourished
for several weeks.
A lot of the time
I take naps,
because changes
make me tired
and my body is
changing quickly.

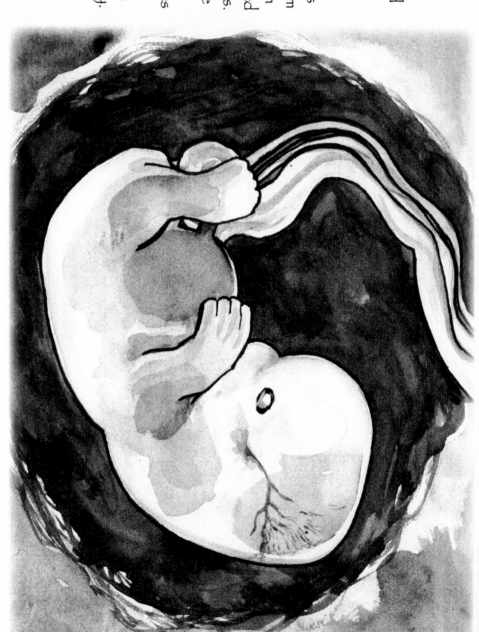

My stubby arms and legs grow longer, and I have feet with toes and hands and fingers. I can open and close my eyes and mouth, and sometimes I like to suck my thumb.

The sounds familiar to me are Mom's slowly pulsating tummy, the beating of her heart, my own smaller heartbeat, her voice, and Dad's voice. Sometimes I hear music and my dog's bark. I like all these sounds and I'm so happy as I grow bigger.

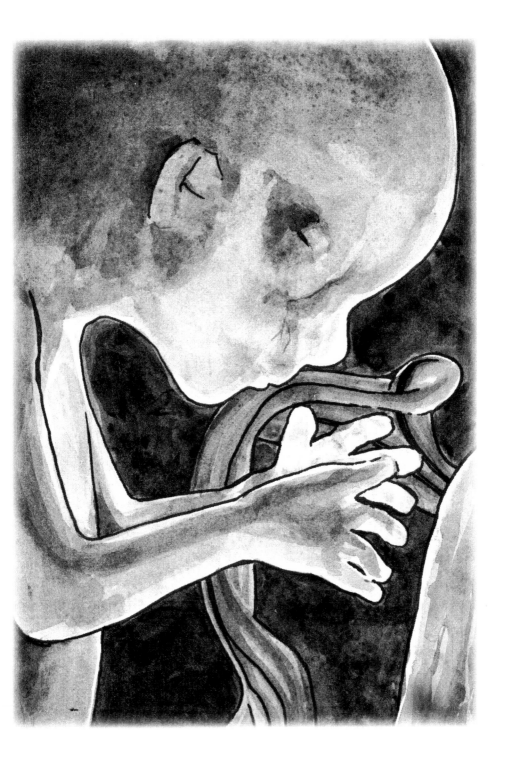

Then strange things happen. Mom becomes very still and sometimes I hear her cry. Her voice and Dad's sound worried. In a few days there are loud, roaring sounds and many voices around us. I'm confused and don't know what's happening.

Soon we are all flying over the mountains to a big city where the hospital has special doctors and nurses. The trip lasts about three hours, then Mom becomes very still again and we both rest. After all that noise, I take a good long nap and feel better.

26 Weeks Old

A few days later, I am feeling very comfortable in Mom's warm, fluid, dark womb with food coming to me through the tube in my tummy. Suddenly, more new voices surround Mom and Dad and there's a lot of activity. In the middle of a dark winter's night, Mom has an operation because she is very sick. The doctors and nurses help me be born. My, how my world changes!

This outside world is very strange and full of mystery.

Voices are much louder; there are bright lights and cool breezes. Several hands help me take my first breaths. Others wash me and check my whole body carefully. I'm scared, then Mom and Dad's hands touch me for the first time and they both kiss me. I grab mom's finger. It's better then, because I hear the love in their voices. They tell me my name is William Michael. It sounds so good when they say, "Welcome to this big world, Liam."

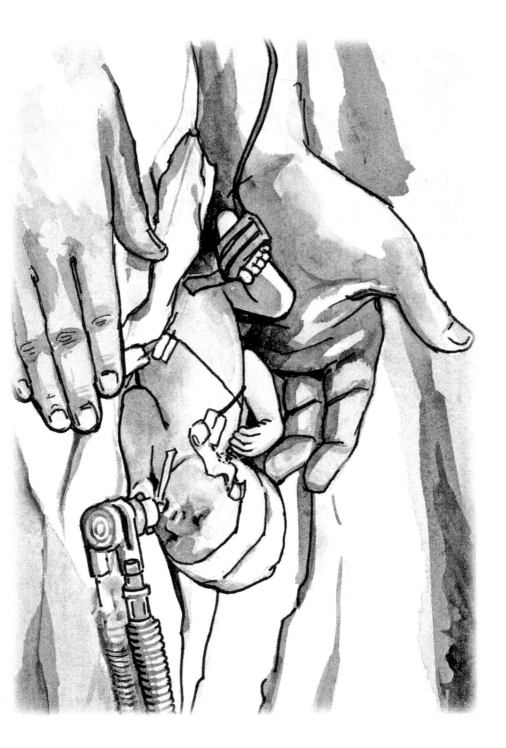

My Birthday and First Home

Since I'm very small, 1 lb. 13 oz., my story is different from most newborns. I'm about the size of a chipmunk and am too small to live on my own, even with Mom and Dad's help. So my life in the NICU begins. The nurses take me to this very special place in the hospital that has good machines that help them take care of lots of babies like me. It's a safe and cozy place and there's a comfortable, tiny bed for me with warm lights and soft pads. This will be my home for many weeks.

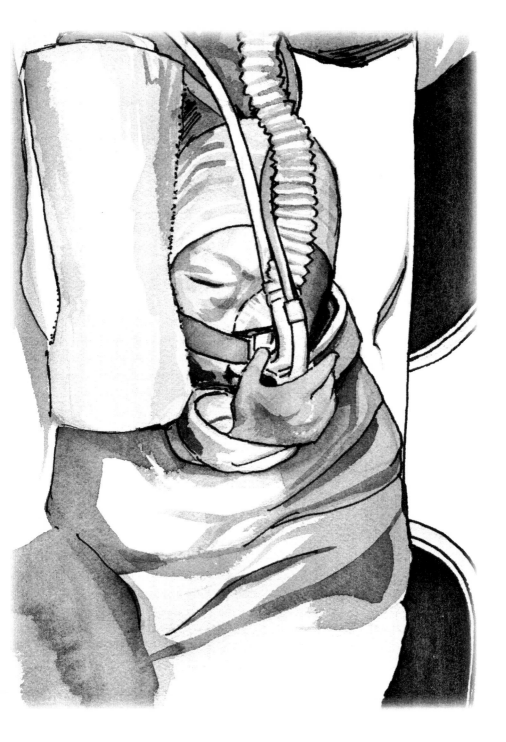

My lungs are too small to keep breathing on my own so a tiny oxygen mask is gently placed over my nose. A warm sensor is taped to my foot to keep track of my heartbeat. A needle pokes into my arm to give me fluid now that my tummy cord is no longer attached to Mom for food. It hurts! There are beeps and buzzers coming from the machines all the time, and I'm very restless. The nurses watch me and the machines carefully.

Soon Dad comes to see me, so I feel lots better.

Then it's time for us all to rest after a very busy night.

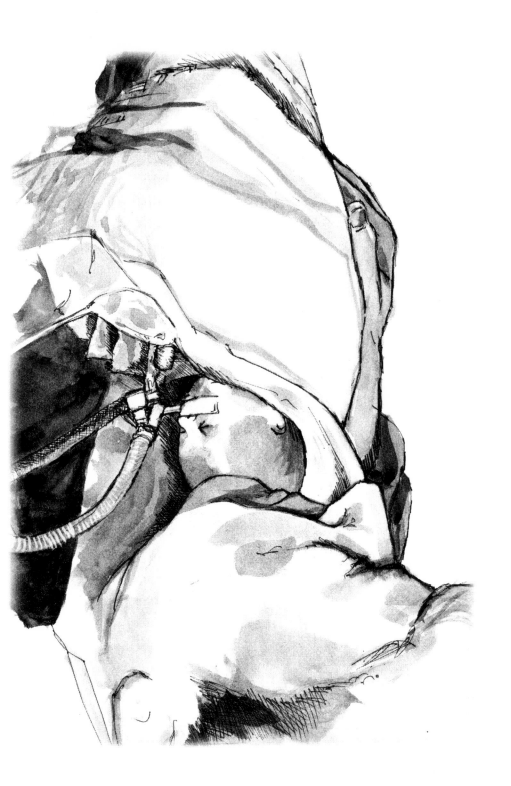

4 Days Old

Now my parents start counting how old I am in a different way, beginning with the day I was born. When I was two days old, Mom came to visit me along with Dad. She was getting better now after being very sick.

When I'm four days old, we get to do my first "Kangaroo Care." Mom or Dad hold me against their chest and sit with me for a couple of hours. It feels very good, almost like being inside Mom's tummy again. They'll take turns doing this each day for many weeks. I love it; it's the best part of my day.

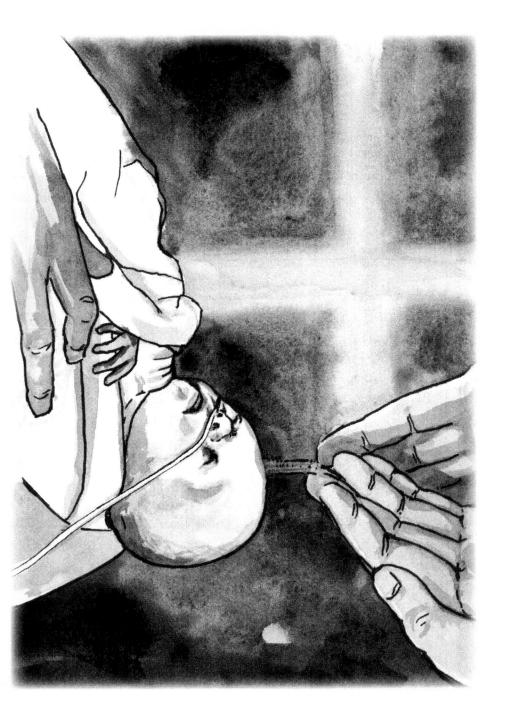

10 Days Old

My first Christmas is a special time to remember when Jesus was born. He was much bigger than me when he was born, but we still have a lot in common. I became even closer to him when I was baptized six days ago.

This Christmas day, I'm glad he was close to me, because I couldn't breathe at all for a while and my heart stopped beating. I was very peaceful, but Jesus gave me strength and helped my nurses get my heart and lungs working again.

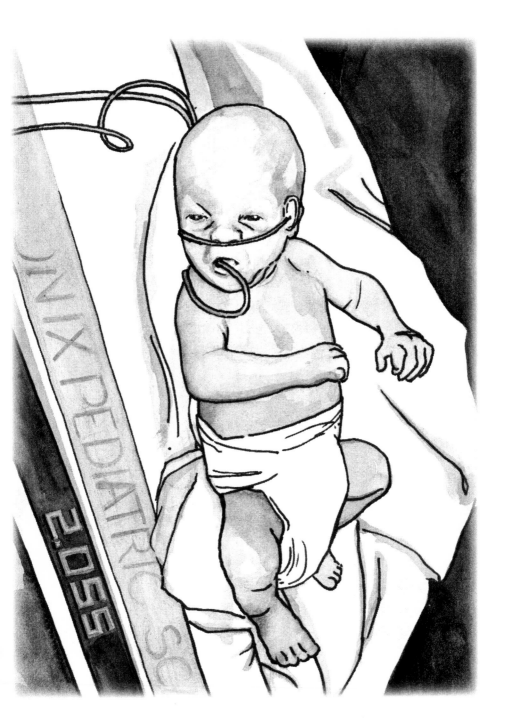

One of my doctors, either Dr. Ben or Dr. Javier, checks me each day and listens to my heart, which has a hole in it. They talk to the nurses and my parents. The nurses turn me over and check my monitors often; they give me good care and medicines to make my heart and lungs stronger. They're my special friends. Mom and Dad take care of me now, too, along with the nurses. They take my temperature and change my diaper and clothes. Many other family members and friends come for brief visits with Mom and Dad.

I now have a tube going down my throat so I can drink Mom's milk, which is best to make me grow big and strong. Sometimes it's very uncomfortable. I lost some ounces of weight my first few days, so it's taking a while for me to grow much bigger than my birth weight. I'm weighed several times each day and am so happy when I hear Mom and Dad and the nurses say I'm bigger.

I weigh 2 lb. 1 oz. today, which is as big as a mom rabbit. The nurses bring me a very special crib called an "isolette." I really like it! It has a cover, adjustable lighting, and an even, warm temperature and humidity. There are holes in one side of it so people can reach their hands in to care for me. All of my IVs have been removed, so now it's up to Mom's milk to help me gain weight. I'm getting some medication for an infection; it goes in the milk I take through my feeding tube, but I only taste the good milk.

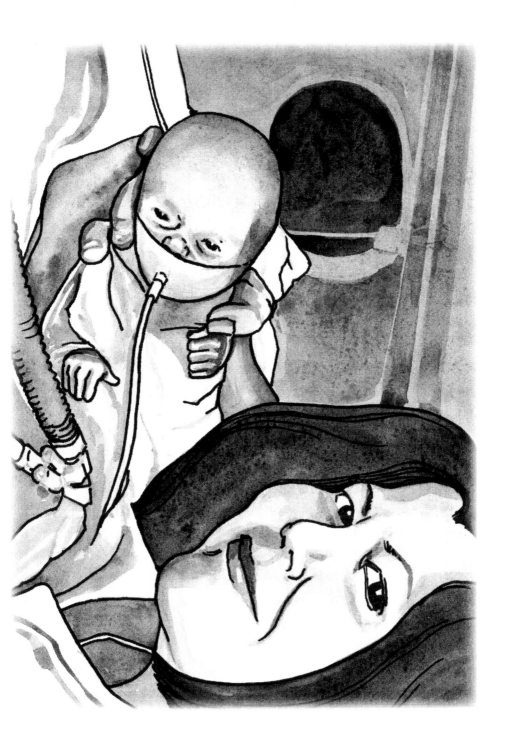

30 Days Old

I'm 2 lb. 7 oz. on my one-month birthday. It's the birthday of one of my favorite nurses, too; her name is Christine. We get our picture taken together. My grandparents come to visit and help celebrate how much I've grown.

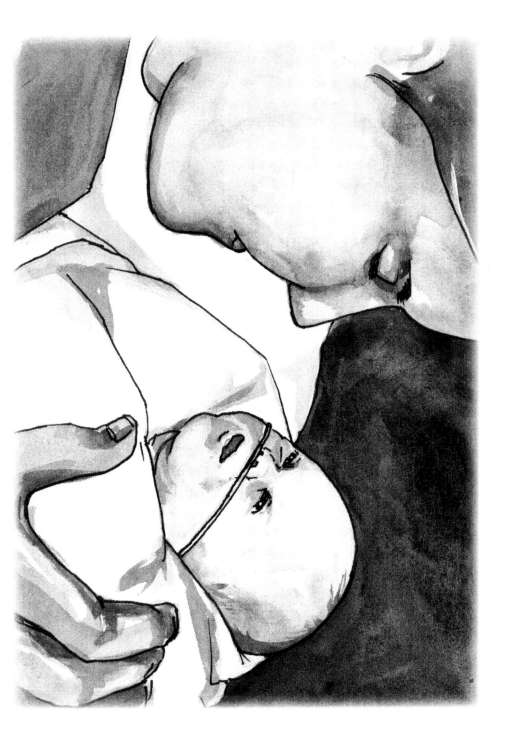

40 Days Old

Sometimes I get to breathe on my own for a little while to help strengthen my lungs, but soon I get my C-PAP (oxygen mask) again because I'm more comfortable when I have it. The very good news today is that I'm now a member of the 3 lb. club!

45 Days Old

My weight is 3 lbs. 5 ozs., which is about as big as a daddy rabbit. I'm off the C-PAP sometimes and am getting lower levels of oxygen through a more comfortable little tube inserted in my nose. I'm breathing well on my own now.

A few days ago, Dr. Ben took a picture of the inside of my head to make sure the bleeding in my brain was healing. Dr. Javier checked my eyes. The doctors do this ever so often to make sure my brain and eyes are healing and growing right. I like it when they come to see me because they are my good friends, too.

60 Days Old

I've grown to be 4 lbs. now and am in a bigger crib that looks more like the one I'll have when I go home. My crib and room are made brighter by things my cousins and friends far away back home have made for me or brought to me. Soft fuzzy toys and a picture of my dog, Eli, are on my crib sides.

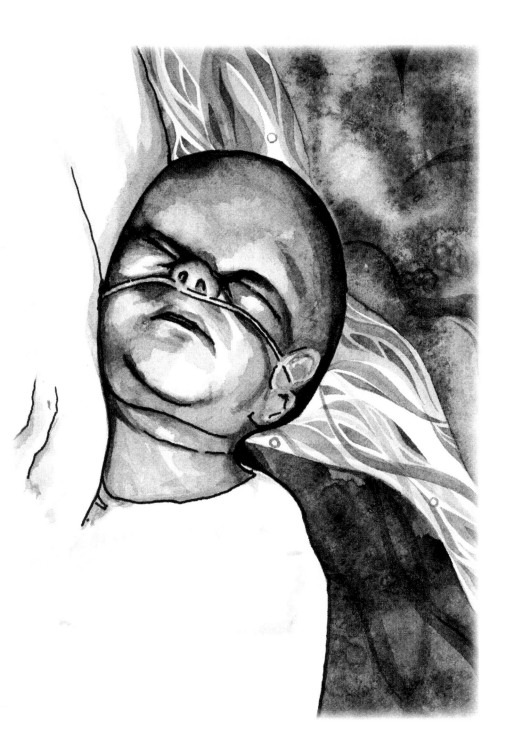

64 Days Old

I've been taking Mom's milk from a bottle for a while, but now I get to nurse from Mom's breast, too. It's good and extra yummy this way; I really like it. I still need the feeding tube sometimes because eating is hard work for me and I fall asleep

before I get enough to help me grow.

Mom and Dad were scared yesterday because I couldn't breathe at all for a few minutes. I returned to a shadowy land and was bathed in a soft golden light for a while. I was surrounded by angels and spirit friends and was not scared at all. The nurses urged me back to life in Mom and Dad's care. My parents

welcomed me back with tears, smiles, pats, and much love,

and I'm happy to be with them, too.

Now I am back on the C-PAP for a while so this doesn't happen again.

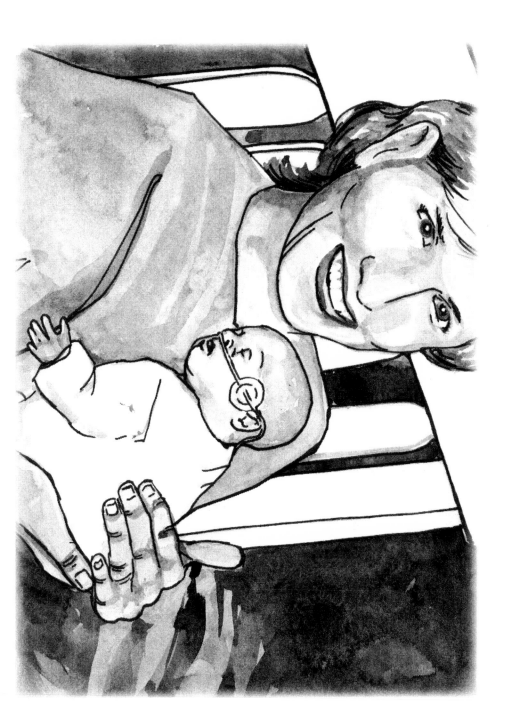

75 Days Old

I'm 5 lbs. now, about as big as a lazy grandpa rabbit. The hole in my heart is almost gone. Happy day! I'm getting lots of visitors now that I'm big enough to be held. It can be uncomfortable for them because they don't know what to do with my tubes and wires. It's great for me, though, because I like meeting new people.

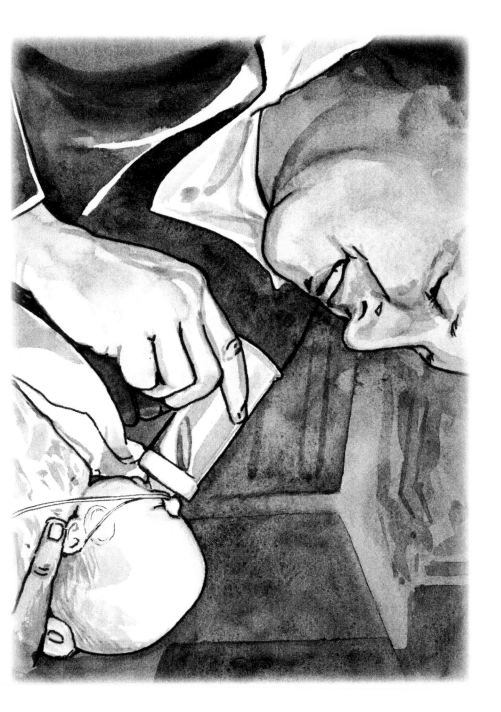

I weigh 6 lb. 3 oz. today. The feeding tube is mostly gone except when I'm too sleepy to eat. I drink milk from Mom or from a bottle. Either Mom or Dad is here all the time now because I eat better for them, but often some of the milk burps back up. I'm getting medicine for this reflux and for high blood pressure. I'm on and off of my low-level oxygen. The nurses still watch my oxygen level very carefully, as well as my heart rate.

105 Days Old

Tomorrow would be Mom's due date if I were still in her tummy. Just as if mine had been a normal birth, she and Dad hope to take me home soon!

Mom and Dad meet with my doctors and nurses today and come up with a pre-dismissal plan. It'll begin in a few days if I continue to gain weight. Today I'm 6 lb. 14 oz, which is as big as lots of newborn people.

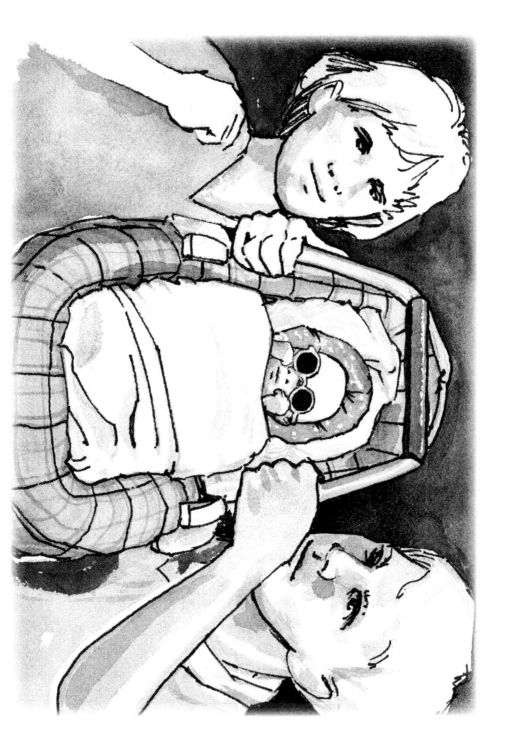

112 Days Old

Job well done! I now weigh 7 lb. 4 oz. It was fun having a car seat trial today, so my oxygen level could be tested while I sat in it.

Today I move out of the NICU into a regular hospital room where Mom and Dad can sleep, too. It's quieter without all the alarms, beeps, and buzzers of the equipment I don't need anymore. This is wonderful; we're a happy family tonight. I like having just Dad and Mom care for me.

113 Days Old

Today I'm 7 lb.
9 oz. and on a
very low level of
oxygen. Doctors
Ben and Javier
come to talk to
Mom and Dad;
then my nurses
come to visit.

They all surprise us with a cake for a going-away party; I even get to taste some icing! We have a fun party with lots of laughing and talking. We're all happy because I will be going home tomorrow.

114 Days Old

My weight is 7 lb. 14 oz. on this happy day. We wave good-bye to all the very special people who have cared for me. Their loving hearts and hands will be missed, but many other friends and family wait for us at home.

And Eli, my dog, is waiting for me, too.

Dad, Mom, and I get in the car and begin the long ride over the mountains to our home. Hooray!

The Artist:

The cover artwork and the illustrations for "William and the NICU" were created by Kevin F. Novack. He is a Catholic Priest of the Diocese of Pueblo, presently serving as Pastor of St. Michael's Parish in Cañon City, CO. He received his Master's of Fine Arts in illustration from Savannah College of Art and Design. Father Novack continues to show his artwork throughout Colorado.

Kevin F. Novack Fine Art